ALL IN THE SAME BOAT

Family Cruising Around the Atlantic

Fiona McCall
and Paul Howard

 ⟦A DOUGLAS GIBSON BOOK⟧

Canadian Cataloguing in Publication Data

McCall, Fiona
  All in the same boat

ISBN 0-7710-5437-8

1. Yachts and yachting – Atlantic Ocean.   2. Voyages and travels – 1951–   . 3. Lorcha (Yacht).
I. Howard, Paul. II. Title.

G530.M22 1988   910'.09163   C88-093883-8

Typeset by Compeer Typographic Services Limited

Printed and bound in Canada by Friesen Printers

A Douglas Gibson Book

McClelland and Stewart
The Canadian Publishers
481 University Avenue
Toronto M5G 2E9

To Gladys of Scotland and Eleanor of Michigan, grandmothers who, no matter toward what far-flung corner of the world we were headed, always had a letter waiting for us.

CONTENTS

PREFACE

amily sailing might bring to your mind a sunny summer day with kids and dog and a picnic lunch in the basket as you head out for an island beach, before a gentle sail brings you back to the marina as the sun goes down.

Crossing an ocean on a small sailboat is just like going out for that day sail – only you keep going.

We set out from Toronto one summer's day and now, several years and many thousands of miles later, we are far from our Toronto marina berth. But we still enjoy feeling *Lorcha* running free before a brisk wind with the family together in the cockpit, and Peter and Penny, only four and six years old when we began this voyage, still eagerly look forward to a picnic on the beach, no matter where that beach or island lies, or what ocean laps its shore.

We've shared many anchorages with other boats and crews, some of whom you'll meet in the following pages. For the most part they're ordinary people like ourselves, but we tell about our own and other voyagers' extra-ordinary adventures, which are as much a part of sailing on the world's oceans as the planning and the navigation. With our tales of history, of how the kids learn to adapt to the yachting life as we sail out of the St. Lawrence Seaway, of how we cope with gale-force winds on our first ocean passage, or of the exhilaration of surfing down the twenty-foot waves as dolphins escort us into harbour in the Cape

Verde Islands, we hope you will get to know our family and get a glimpse of family life afloat.

So step down into *Lorcha*'s cockpit; settle yourself into a comfortable corner and we'll sail together in the wake of pirates and early navigators as we explore the amazing islands of the Atlantic Ocean, or the Amazon jungle, or the underwater delights of Bonaire in the Caribbean.

Just as we planned and completed the trip together as a team, so we have written the book together. You'll find that sometimes the "I" becomes Fiona, at other times Paul. We think that from the context this won't be too confusing. We're simply taking turns relating our adventures, just as we would if you were sitting in the cockpit with us.

There were trials and tribulations, to be sure, and even some dangerous moments when we had only each other to rely on to get us out of a tricky situation. But we have voyaged into a different world that once only lay beyond the distant horizon. If that world beckons to you at all through this book, we shall be well pleased.

We are four very different personalities who have lived in what most people would consider a very small space for a considerable length of time. But as we moved on to new countries, with nights spent gazing at the millions of stars above us and days surrounded by the blue immensity of the ocean, our small space has seemed infinite.

We're all in the same boat – and we wouldn't have it any other way.

Paul Howard and Fiona McCall
March 1988

250 MILES SOUTHEAST OF CAPETOWN

INTRODUCTION

How a Scot born in India and an American from Michigan came to sail around the world with their two Canadian children is a long story.

To keep it short, let's just say that two things brought us together. The first was Canada, which in 1963 lured Fiona from a humdrum job in London into the world of Toronto theatre (where, among other things, she worked for a year promoting the hit musical *Hair*) and the high-pressure advertising arena, where her company's clients included DuPont and General Motors. Paul in turn left the United States to settle in Toronto armed with his Master of Social Work degree in 1972. This was after a spell in the Peace Corps, first in Biafra until civil war hit his area, then in Togo, establishing fish-culture stations and breaking wild donkeys to harness, thus introducing animal traction to the area. (Not so very far from the world of theatre, when you come to think of it.)

The second thing to bring us together was a small advertisement Fiona spotted in one of the papers.

"Toronto Yacht Club. Chinese junk in harbour offers opportunity to sail all summer for $150."

Paul was already part of the junk's crew; after catching the sailing bug at university, he was so keen to get on the water again (sailing had been poor among the wild donkeys) that he had made a deal with the junk's owner to do woodworking and maintenance in return for a summer's sailing. And then, rushing down to the harbour to take advantage of the fabulous offer in the paper, came this interesting lady named Fiona, a novice but obviously a keen sailor. . . .

It wasn't long before we became the TYC's first serious romance.

The sailing soon became just as serious. After a summer on Lake Ontario in a 19-foot plywood sloop with no engine – once, greatly daring, we made a 400-mile trip to the Thousand Islands and back – we began to lay very ambitious plans. Ever since he had hitchhiked around Europe, Paul had dreamed of some day coming back to cruise the canals and rivers that thread through so much of the Continent. We began to save and prepare for just such a trip, taking navigation classes and learning all we could about sailing from magazines, books, and the practical experience of boat-handling in the summers.

In May 1975, two years after we'd met, we flew to England to buy a boat.

Seagull was a 30-foot gaff cutter, seventy-two years old and of wooden construction. She had been out of the water for two years and needed extensive repairs and updating. But the price was right at $3,000 – and another $3,000 took care of the cockpit-rebuilding, a new diesel engine, and two new sails. Then it was Eastward Ho! across the Channel and into the Dutch, Belgian, and French canal systems. Blissfully we wended our way through small canals, large rivers, scores of locks, little villages, main cities, waterside markets, mountain tunnels, and more locks, enjoying the ever-changing picturesque countryside – not to mention the daily doses of pâté, fromage, pain au chocolat, and wonderful and varied wines. It's a trip we'd choose to repeat again any day, and was certainly an ideal gentle introduction to life on the water, if not the ocean.

We soon reached the Mediterranean and ambled along the French coast before cutting back inland towards the Bay of Biscay, where we experienced our first gale.

"Gale force imminent or already in progress in North Biscay," said the 6 p.m. British Broadcasting Corporation weather forecaster, shortly after we had set out from the port of Royan into North Biscay.

We looked at each other.

"We've never been in a gale before," said Fiona brightly. "Let's just stay out and sail through it."

This proved to be a very silly idea. During our first gale, we lost our inflatable dinghy, ruined our radio and binoculars with salt water, and allowed ourselves to be "pooped": we had left the companionway hatch open and a big breaking wave filled the interior of our boat to bunk level. We were in no real danger, because we were quickly able to pump the water out, but it was certainly an unpleasant experience! We didn't even get nearer to our destination. After sailing two hundred miles both against (north) and then running before (south) the wind, two days of hard sailing landed us back in the port we had set out from.

The only good thing about the experience was that we came through it tired out but relatively unscathed. The lessons learned when sailing through your first gale have to be absorbed some time, but you really have to hope that that first heavy-weather experience will neither be too bad nor last too long.

Around this time we realized that if we wanted to do a trip down the River Danube, *Seagull* was unsuitable. Her five-foot draft was too deep and she was too heavy and cumbersome to handle in fast river currents and difficult locking situations. So we sold her in La Rochelle and ordered a Kingfisher 20 + from England. *Lady Fiona* was a new fibreglass twin-keeler, 21 feet 6 inches long, with the junk rig, a sail plan that our reading suggested was worth trying, and to which (after Toronto) we were sentimentally attached. We had *Lady Fiona* trucked from England to the headwaters of the Danube in Regensburg, north of Munich, and proceeded to float down the River Danube with her in fine style, enjoying the different lifestyles in Germany, Austria, Czechoslovakia, Hungary (where we put up the mast), Yugoslavia, Romania, and Bulgaria, before eventually arriving in the Black Sea.

Now in our second year of travel, we felt it was time to make our way down the Black Sea coast through Romania, Bulgaria, and Turkey to Istanbul. This was our first experience of overnight sails, and it was made a little unnerving because all coast lights in Romania and Bulgaria were put out at night. But

Turkey proved to be one of the most hospitable countries we have ever visited, and we spent every night ashore as someone's guest, whether for dinner or for just a cup of coffee.

After a spectacular passage down the Bosphorus, we wanted to linger in Istanbul, but as the weather worsened and the winds from the north grew colder, we moved south to the Greek Islands, settling in Piraeus for a few weeks. It was probably the idyllic atmosphere that did it, but we began thinking of having a family and – in the distant future – of taking that family sailing. Who knew but that some day we might even start sailing across oceans with our children?

"First things first," said Fiona. "Either we get pregnant now, or we cross the Atlantic Ocean in *Lady Fiona*. As far as I'm concerned, either would be a great adventure."

She set about things just as methodically as when she was preparing for the European cruise, and there was a great deal of looking at dates and temperature-taking, until six weeks later we happily knew we were pregnant.

It was time to arrange passage home for both us and *Lady Fiona*.

As the youngest of the twelve passengers on the 5,000-ton cargo vessel (not to mention having our own boat as deck cargo), we enjoyed a special relationship with the crew, and spent most of our time on the bridge doing sextant sights along with the ship's navigator. Before our 45-day trip to Florida was over, we were both able to place the ship within a couple of miles of the navigator's position, and the lessons learned on that voyage were to stand us in good stead.

By April we were sailing up the Intracoastal Waterway back to Canada via New York and the Hudson River, Fiona practising her Lamaze natural-childbirth exercises in the cockpit and both of us wondering if the baby would be born before or after we got to Toronto.

Also under discussion was how big our next boat would have to be and when we might be ready to start another trip.

"But for that, of course," said Fiona smilingly, "we'll need a crew of two. . . ."

4

"Sailors Beat Stork" read the headlines over the pictures that appeared in all three Toronto daily newspapers. From the U.S. side of Lake Ontario we had phoned some friends to tell them when we would be arriving at Toronto's Pier 4, and word had spread among our newspaper friends until there was a crowd of photographers to greet us and take pictures of a nine-months-pregnant Fiona as she stepped ashore.

After our pictures appeared in the newspapers, we were both offered several jobs. Fiona chose to do some free-lance publicity work for Harbourfront, Toronto's exciting new waterfront-development project, and happily plunged into her old public-relations lifestyle again, not a whit slowed down by the fact that the baby was due in a couple of weeks.

Meanwhile we lived on board our tiny ship, now named "the Baby Boat", which was moored in Toronto Harbour, right alongside Fiona's new workplace.

Sure enough, two weeks later Penny was born.

Paul chose not to work for a while, as he wanted to look after the baby, and to repair and sell the house we had rented out while we had been away. That house was no good to us any more, as it had no backyard in which we could build a new boat! So after selling *Lady Fiona* he would be looking for a large backyard with house attached.

We found the backyard, and the house that came attached to it was a hundred years old and sadly in need of renovation. Paul carted Penny about, her little face peeping from his chest pouch as he dodged between wall studs and pipes to direct the renovation work. While Fiona worked at Harbourfront helping to transform Toronto's bleak waterfront into a place crowded with visitors, Paul wrote articles, reviews, and a book on furniture design, and looked after Penny. When Penny was two, her brother Peter was born. Now the crew was complete, and all we needed was a boat.

LORCHA

Choosing the perfect boat and outfitting it for cruising is a confusing and awesome task. When you're planning to cruise around the world with small children, the task is even harder. For the boat will be your home as well as a means of transportation. The trouble is, the more magazines and books you read on how to choose the ideal boat, the more confused you're likely to become. Designers and boat-builders spout numbers of minimum tonnes of displacement per crew, minimum waterline length, maximum sail sizes, and various ratios and numbers.

Fiona and I tend to think of boats in terms of the minimum size we can be comfortable with when travelling, living in harbour, or scrubbing and painting the bottom. It's all a matter of opinion, as we learned when we discussed it with our cruising friends:

"We would never again build a vessel this big for the four of us," said Joan on the 56-foot schooner she and her husband had built for themselves and their two young daughters. They had decided on a vessel large enough to give them room for all the conveniences of a home ashore. . . .

"She's a good vessel, but next time I want a more modern hull and at least ten feet more in length," said Ricco of his fifty-year-old 55-foot wooden schooner. The usual complement on Board *Yawim* was Ricco, his wife, Gitta, and three children aged six to eleven, along with

Choice of vessel . . . minimum size . . . specific needs . . .
steel hull . . . sail plan . . . engine . . . self-steering . . .
comfortable bunks . . . junk rig . . . backyard builder . . .
children's fittings . . . safety harnesses . . . stowage . . .
life raft . . . fuel . . . anchors . . . galley . . . water

---

a dog and a cat. On their last Atlantic crossing, they had a crew of ten.

"*Eryngo* is the perfect vessel for family sailing," said Andy of his 40-foot aft-cabin ketch. "Even with Caroline and the three kids [aged seven, five, and one and a half years] on board, we often take on an extra crew member for long passages and still have plenty of room." The Van Herks have now completed a nine-year circumnavigation.

When I started to plan our new boat, I outlined our needs as follows:

1. We needed a steel hull for watertight integrity and security, especially in coral-strewn waters.

2. We needed a directionally stable hull, with a comfortable motion and moderate displacement, so that a relatively small rig and light gear would drive her.

3. We needed an easily handled sail plan, rigged for single-handing as there would be only one person on watch at a time. That person should be able to reef and do all sail handling. For us, this meant the Chinese lug or "junk" sail plan.

4. We needed reliable diesel power. We originally built our backyard boat with only an outboard on a bracket at the transom to save money and give us more interior space. But this was a poor decision, and we changed our minds before we set out and opted to install a reliable inboard diesel.

5. We needed strong self-steering gear which would be able to relieve us of steering duties in any weather. Two people simply cannot hand-steer for passages that average ten or twelve exhausting days.

6. We needed three good, dry berths, comfortable under any conditions in harbour or at sea. Only three bunks are needed at sea, as we keep a 24-hour watch and either Fi or I are always out in the cockpit. We also wanted a double bunk for use in harbour, where Fi and I could have some togetherness.

(In Appendix C, *Choosing a Boat*, I write about the pros and cons of these factors, which may be helpful to anyone thinking of building or buying a boat for cruising.)

In the end we chose a double-chine steel boat just over twenty-nine feet long and named her *Lorcha*. We had come across this singularly appropriate name by chance in the dictionary. A "lorcha" was a type of eighteenth-century Portuguese vessel, used in the trade from Portugal to the Orient, which had a western hull and a Chinese sail – akin to our own Dutch-designed hull with its modern adaptation of the Chinese junk rig. At five tonnes displacement she was in the moderate-displacement range. And perhaps moderate is the key description of her shape. She has a long fin keel of just over four foot draft, and a strong skeg in front of the rudder, which hangs at the aft end of the waterline. She has some overhang, a nice buoyant stern, and a reasonably wide beam. Designed by Frans Coblens of Amsterdam in 1977 and built in series production as a KM 30 in Hamilton, Ontario, by Karmac Yachts, she represents what I call a mild-mannered cruising yacht of a recent type. (For further details on *Lorcha* and her equipment, see Appendix A.)

At under thirty feet on deck, *Lorcha* is small for a four-person ocean-cruising vessel, yet with two small children and two compatible adults, she has done us well. She is junk-rigged (our own mixture of a Blondie Hasler rig and a Gallant rig) with a free-standing mast, and she gives us a good turn of speed. We regularly average over 100 miles a day on long passages, and sometimes log 120 to 130 miles in twenty-four hours. For a vessel of only 23 feet 7 inches on the waterline, this is very respectable.

But all of this was very much in the future the never-to-be-forgotten winter's day when the bare steel hull was delivered to our backyard. After months of planning, I had decided to outfit *Lorcha* myself, building in the interior and putting the rig together. So I covered her with a tarpaulin and installed a small wood-burning stove, and Penny and I began working on *Lorcha's* interior.

From the first day she scrambled on board, Penny loved the boat. It was the biggest, best, most exciting toy a kid could wish for; there were scraps of wood to bang together, fascinating tools to play with, corners to hide in, and wood shavings to throw all over the place. She was soon fearless about scaling the ladder, and even when we took it down she still tried to get on board. By the spring, whenever less-than-two-years-old Penny was missing, we only had to look in the boat.

"This will be your bunk, Penny," we would tell her. And with a few cooing noises she would crawl in, contentedly playing with her bits of sawn-off scraps as I sawed and set screws. There was no doubt about the high point of her day – working with her dad on *Lorcha*!

As Peter grew older, he followed in Penny's footsteps, loving the boat and being quite at home in it, happily banging away with his own little set of plastic work tools. He could scale the ten-foot boat ladder before he could walk, and at less than one year old he too considered the boat interior his best playground.

Doesn't *everyone* have a boat in their backyard?

I'm sometimes asked what special things I did to fit out the boat for the use of small children – and by that I don't mean as a playground in the backyard.

I had the stanchions, pushpit, and pulpit – the vertical on-deck fittings to which the lifelines that run around the boat are attached – made thirty inches high, with double lifelines. (The stanchions are the along-deck "posts", and the pulpit is made up of curved posts and pipes at the bow, and the pushpit of posts and curved pipes at the stern.) Lifelines are comparable to a safety fence and help prevent people from falling overboard, and the double lifelines were made too high for a child to go over accidentally. We had originally intended putting netting on the lifelines, but as the children were already four and six by the time we moved on board, and quite used to being on the boat, we never did install it. But we did place handholds around the boat at a height that children can reach.

For further safety on deck, we installed large ring-bolts at the companionway where the children could clip on the hooks of their safety harnesses before actually leaving the companionway. We taught the children to be responsible for their own safety as early as we could.

"Peter, go down below and get your safety harness" proved to be an oft-heard cry on our first few days on the ocean, until both children clipped themselves on automatically.

Most production boats have interiors designed for adults of average height, which means that the galley counter and sinks are too high for children to help at, or even to wash their hands. Small children need a secured step installed here, as they do in the head, which will usually be mounted too high for them to use without help; here handholds at a child's level are very useful indeed.

I had our cockpit dodger made extra large so that the whole family could sit there protected from rain, spray, or the sun. Because we have the junk rig, we have no sheet winches at the cockpit coamings, leaving the forward end of the cockpit clear and well protected.

As for bunks, this is an area of vital importance, where I spent a lot of planning and building time getting things right. Many production boats have bunks on an angle to the fore-and-aft line of the vessel. This makes the vessel seem more roomy, but these neatly angled bunks are a misery at sea. On long passages you may spend as much as two weeks heeled over on the same tack. You can imagine what sleeping is like on an angled bunk, when the boat is heeled with your feet well above your head, or vice versa. Unless you plan to spend all your nights sleeping in harbour, avoid angled bunks (incidentally, stowage under such a bunk is minimal, as it is pushed against the side of the hull with no liner to keep the contents safe from hull condensation).

So I built our bunks straight fore and aft, with a hull liner and plenty of space under them. (For maximum comfort, bunks should, of course, be planned for the aft two-thirds of the boat.)

10

Built out parallel to the centreline of the vessel, the bunks are likely to be out in the air more, which is a blessing in the tropics, where small bulk-headed cabins are stifling. I made sure to allow a hatch and an opening port for each cabin so that air could circulate. The opening ports in the children's quarterberths open into the cockpit footwell and are rarely closed, allowing air to circulate over the sleeping kids.

The curved outboard side of the children's bunks is built up with cubbyholes for their toys and clothing, making the berths properly narrow. Wide berths might be nice in port, but too wide a berth at sea can leave the luckless occupant rolling about, sleeping fitfully if at all.

During the day, children play about in their bunks, so we were careful about what we stowed around the area, since a falling child will grasp at anything to regain his balance, not realizing that a wire may pull out. We kept other dangerous equipment, such as easily triggered fire extinguishers or flares, well out of reach, and carefully rounded all corners on shelves to avoid bumped heads.

As I built, I arranged for some convenient stowage near their bunks for the toys they would play with there, and provided a place for games, books, crayons, etc., near the salon table where they would be used. If the children's things were easily to hand when we were at sea, we knew that it would be much easier for the children to be independent and occupy themselves.

As for the adults, a double bunk on a family boat is a requirement. If there is no place for the partners to have a cuddle or sleepy contented conversation, how can you maintain a family? I built ours as an athwartships convertible dinette just forward of the galley. It could also be used as a lounging area at sea, especially by Penny and Peter if the seas were rough.

But we knew that far more important than the physical arrangements made for the children is the attitude of the skipper and the mate towards the needs of young crew. Their comfort and well-being is pivotal.

"Can you reef a couple of panels during lunch?" Fiona would

sometimes ask. "It's baked beans, and it would be easier for the kids if we slow down for half an hour."

A contented and comfortable crew, no matter what their ages, is a good crew, and we well knew that our plans for long-distance ocean sailing would all fall apart if the children were not happy.

Years of careful saving and preparation passed, with Fiona working at Harbourfront and me writing and working on *Lorcha*, while Penny and Peter worked at growing, at which they were very good. In due course, when Penny was about three and Peter an energetic fourteen months, *Lorcha* was ready for the move from the backyard (which looked unbelievably empty and strange without her) into the water.

After day-sailing around Toronto and a few passages across Lake Ontario, we knew we had the boat we wanted. Our major decisions on what to carry for a trip around the world had been made.

Though we considered our dinghy to be adequate as a lifeboat for inshore sailing, for example, we decided a life raft was necessary for this trip. Though *Lorcha* was as strong and seaworthy as I could make her, I couldn't bear the thought of our family not having a second chance of survival. So our four-man raft was stored in the cockpit.

Combined diesel-fuel tankage and jerry cans provided a capacity of 200 litres, enough for 100 hours of motoring at 4.5 knots. We carried 5 litres each of kerosene for lamps and gasoline for the 2-h.p. dinghy outboard. We stowed 5 litres of engine oil – enough for two oil changes – and carried two 10-pound propane cooking-gas bottles, which last for about three months.

We carried four anchors ranging from 17 to 35 pounds, as well as 200 feet of ⅜″ chain and a windlass for the main (7.5-kilo Bruce) anchor, and 30 to 50 feet of chain for each of the others, as well as two 240-foot 12mm-diameter nylon anchor rodes and a 100-footer.

Our L-shaped galley occupied four feet of fore-and-aft space just forward of the port quarterberth. The gimballed cooker was

12

located forward, so the cook wearing the galley bum strap did not have to stand in front of boiling-hot liquids. The pots were to the cook's right hand, and I had added five pounds of lead to the bottom of our gimballed stove to slow its motion. We kept our dishes and pans in racks, and a deck prism helped light the area.

A foot-pump sea-water tap and a hand-pump fresh-water tap were installed at the single sink. I knew that the sea-water tap would be very convenient for washing up and for our other non-drinking water needs. We carried about 340 litres of fresh water, and were to find that we used about 5 litres a day at sea.

Those days at sea were getting closer all the time. Finally we had a date. We would set off down the St. Lawrence Seaway and around the Atlantic Ocean on *Lorcha* on July 1, 1983.

GETTING AWAY

2

Ending one lifestyle and starting another is never easy. I had intended to quit work just three months before our departure date, but I loved my job as Communications Director of Harbourfront and there were several projects I felt I just had to see through, with the result that I managed to stop working only four weeks before we were due to up-anchor.

At least the kids will be in day care until we set sail, I thought, but then Penny fell and broke her arm, and though she went back to her Senior Kindergarten classes after a week, I felt she couldn't manage her usual afternoon day care as well.

Paul was working night and day to add the finishing touches to *Lorcha* and to buy and stow all the supplies. Then, since simply dropping out of your life for two or three years is a little complex, we had to dash about, renting our house, paying taxes, and arranging house insurance, as well as selling our car (who needs a car on the high seas?) and most of our furniture. We also had to meet with our bank manager to arrange a line of credit, and to make sure our boat-ownership papers and our passports were in order.

We whipped everyone into the doctor's office two weeks before we left for necessary shots like tetanus, polio, yellow fever, and typhoid. Unfortunately, this meant that the kids had to endure a large number of injections in a short time, leaving Peter in particular very

14

Quitting jobs . . . broken arm . . . house arrangements . . . necessary
shots . . . Toronto Harbour . . . 400th-anniversary celebrations . . .
Lake Ontario . . . first watch . . . swollen ankles . . . seasick kids . . .
the Murray Canal . . . Kingston at last

---

apprehensive about ever seeing our friendly doctor again.

The day before our departure, Paul had to run across town to pick up two different kinds of malaria pills to take with us, while I tried to track down in which particular filing cabinet at which particular friend's house we had left all our passports and $1,000 in American dollars "safely" locked up. And of course there were farewells from all of the friends, many of whom, I'm sure, were amazed that we were actually going, that our eccentric dream of sailing on the world's oceans with our young children was really going to happen.

Sure enough, on July 1 our friends were out in force at Harbourfront and Peter was hugging his favourite people, Unk-Unk and Aunty Carol, as though he would never see them again. Penny, meanwhile, was holding a huge chocolate birthday cake, which Ron and Gloria Joiner had battled through Canada Day afternoon traffic to present to her. It was, after all, her sixth birthday.

Among the crowd was Ray Woodley, who had wangled three days off work to sail the first leg with us, undeterred by the litter of garbage bags full of provisions and gear still lying in the cockpit waiting to be stowed away. But, ready or not, it was time to go.

"Come on, everybody," said Paul. "I want to get sailing before it's dark. Penny and Peter, into the cockpit; Fiona, take the mooring lines – and Ray, can you fend us off?"

Paul backed *Lorcha* out of the slip and Penny gave three toots on the ship's horn to warn passing traffic there was a vessel coming into Toronto Harbour. Then I took the helm as Paul raised our distinctive seven-panel Chinese lug sail, and a cheer went up from our friends and the crowd of fascinated bystanders on the dock.

A pleasant fifteen-knot westerly was rippling the surface of the water as we sailed out of the Eastern Gap between the city and the crescent of the Toronto Islands, our red sails glowing in the sunset. The wind freshened as we entered Lake Ontario proper and Paul reefed a panel. It was lovely to be sailing fast on what Henry James had called "a great inland ocean", but for our first few days I would have preferred less wind and calmer waters. As it was, there was a nasty chop and I hoped it would not upset Peter and Penny too much. But the wind continued to increase and we soon reefed another panel.

"I can see some of the other boats," said Paul, pointing ahead, and I thought about some advantages of our voyage. Not only were we getting the "practice" of a mini-voyage down an inland waterway – albeit a mighty big one like Lake Ontario and the St. Lawrence Seaway – before we made our first ocean passages, but we were doing so in the company of fifteen other yachts.

A year previously, Paul had read about David Ker, a sailor and retired publisher from Dundas, Ontario. Ker, we learned, was organizing a group of boats to sail down the St. Lawrence to celebrate the four-hundredth anniversary of the landing in Newfoundland in 1583 of one Sir Humphrey Gilbert – an English sailing adventurer who promptly claimed the "new found land" for the King of England, thereby starting the whole of England's far-reaching colonization program.

Ker was looking for boats to join his expedition, and the only restrictions seemed to be a real wish to do the trip and ownership of a vessel at least thirty feet in length. The fleet would leave the Royal Hamilton Yacht Club on July 1, 1983, to arrive in St. John's Harbour on August 3, a tough, but not impossible, schedule.

One of the hard things about leaving home for a long cruise is setting the departure date, which can be put off and put off for any and many legitimate reasons. Not only did the St. Lawrence trip sound interesting – we had done very little sailing in Canada outside Ontario, and sailing as part of a fleet of yachts sounded like fun – but we would now have a definite date to work towards.

But when we phoned him to volunteer, Ker was dubious.

"I really want boats of over 30 feet," he said. "We have to keep on the move if we're going to get to St. John's by August 3. There's going to be a big reception for the fleet on that day and we can't afford to be a minute late. Your boat's only 29 feet 6 inches and most of the other boats will be 35 to 40 feet. I don't know if you'll be able to keep up."

He was also worried about our not taking crew.

"There are lots of locks and a lot of overnight sailing. Most of the boats will have three to five people on board. I don't think two people will be enough."

"Oh, that's all right," we chorused. "We'll have the two children with us."

We didn't feel it was the appropriate moment to point out that Peter and Penny, the sturdy crew who would see us through, were four and six. It worked.

Now here we were on Lake Ontario, having joined the eight boats that had left Hamilton that morning, the Newfoundland flag stretching itself in the wind behind us and the tricolour streamer that all the fleet boats were sporting streaming from a halyard. We and one other boat had come from Toronto, and five other vessels were due to join us along the way at either Kingston or Montreal.

The first leg of the trip was the 200-mile (two-day) sail from Toronto to Kingston, where the boats would rendezvous. Usually when we start out on a trip we'd rather not be too ambitious. Better to sail a few miles to a safe anchorage and spend a day sorting out the last-minute supplies and putting the boat in order. A 48-hour, two-day sail was quite a tall order for the start of a long voyage.

The Lake Ontario shoreline we were following was not especially dramatic – once we left the sprawl of Toronto and its high-rises it soon became fairly flat coastline dotted with the lights of farmhouses and small towns – but it was not without its

17

historical appeal. For until well on in the nineteenth century, the route we were sailing had been Canada's main highway for settlers. And all of the little towns along "the Front" were the centres for the pioneers who headed off with axe and plough up the survey tracts drawn up by the original surveyors away from the lake into the bush. One of these little towns, Cobourg, was of special interest to Paul. In the nineteenth century his great-grandfather had owned and skippered a trading schooner sailing from Cobourg to the New York shore.

Both Penny and Peter were up and too excited to sleep when Ray and I took the first nightwatch from 9 p.m. to 1 a.m. It would be a long night of hand-steering. We hadn't sailed the boat that much – and I'd been so busy that I hadn't handled it at all since it had been launched. Now handling the heavy boat in the strong wind and three-foot swells was difficult and tiring. With our course at approximately 90 degrees, the boat surged first to 120 degrees and then to 60 degrees under my inexpert helmsmanship.

Lorcha had too much motion for sleep to be possible when I did come off watch – and at 4 a.m. I was up again, with my ankles swollen to twice their size, to take my turn at the helm once more. I was exhausted. I knew that getting back into the voyaging habit would be our first challenge.

There are many people who, having saved for, planned, and thought about the cruising life for many years, manage to achieve the pinnacle of actually sailing away. But after all that expense, energy, and commitment, the new adventurers give up after only a few months. For the radical change of lifestyle can be a tough challenge, as my extreme discomfort after only twelve hours demonstrated. My ankles were aching abominably and already my stomach was feeling queasy. The question was not whether we would make our proposed 12,000-mile voyage round the islands of the Atlantic Ocean – but whether we would survive the initial 1,500-mile leg to St. John's, Newfoundland.

At 6 a.m. Peter woke up and wanted to come into the cockpit with me.

"Lie down," I tried to whisper. "Daddy's still asleep."

18

Too late. By then everyone was awake – and both Peter and Penny were looking green. Paul gave Penny a drink of apple juice (probably one of the worst things to give anybody who's feeling queasy) before I could stop him. And the next minute I was juggling with the helm and trying to hold a bucket under a vomiting Penny. At 9 a.m. both kids were asleep again – the best thing that could have happened.

"Let's go the inshore route at the Bay of Quinte," said Paul quietly. "The other boats will all get to Kingston before us – but this is pretty hard on the kids."

I agreed, and we headed for Presqu'ile and the Murray Canal past the Carrying Place, whose name showed its importance to canoeing Indians and voyageurs. Three hours later we were sailing sedately along the calm inland waters and both kids were up, fully recovered and chattering away.

Peter was particularly fascinated by a fast moth that flew alongside the boat, matching our speed.

"How does it do that, Mummy?" he asked. And I smiled as I remembered the people who had said anxiously, "But what about the children's schooling?"

As no one had had much sleep the night before, we decided to tie up for the night at Picton. It looked like a nice old town, but we weren't interested in walking around it – just in having a good night's rest. We tied up at 9 p.m., had a supper of brown rice and stew at 9:30 p.m., and were all in bed and asleep by ten o'clock.

We were up again at 5 a.m., but the seven hours' sleep had done wonders for all of us. We felt energetic and refreshed and were treated to a magical morning mist that coated the channels in front of us, only to be burnt off by a brilliant orange sunrise as we motored through the still waters.

By early afternoon we were approaching the spires of Kingston, a fine grey limestone city steeped in history. It was here that Canada's first prime minister, Sir John A. Macdonald, came to settle as a small boy in 1821 ("In those days they came usually by boat," his biography begins, recounting his arrival in Kingston). Long before then its natural harbour had attracted the French explorers, and the fearless old cavalier Frontenac himself had come up the river from Quebec to build a stronghold there in 1673. But for the proximity of the potentially troublesome United States just across the Lake, Kingston could have been Canada's capital. With its fine harbour and its grand old grey buildings (overlooked by Fort Henry, flanked by Hangman's Bay and Deadman's Bay), it was a suitable historic rendezvous for our historic fleet's voyage.

We were in Kingston by early afternoon and at last met some of our companion boats. No matter that we were the last boat in – the schedule gave us a day and overnight here, so we had a chance to get fully rested, although we chose to go to the evening wine-and-cheese party offered to the fleet by the Mayor of Kingston. This, of course, is a city of knowledgeable sailors, which had played host to the sailing events in the 1976 Olympics.

We had, in fact, travelled for more than double the length of time it took the fastest boat to sail the first leg. Keith Burley and his crew aboard *Genevieve II* had sailed the distance in an astonishing eighteen hours, and had obviously revelled in the windy weather.

We were just glad to be in port, and in good spirits.

SAILING THROUGH HISTORY

3

When we set out from Kingston we left the broad familiar waters of Lake Ontario and plunged at once into the current of the St. Lawrence River. The change was dramatic. For here the granite strip of the ancient Canadian Shield sweeps down to the river from the north, leaving the tips of countless islands scattered in the stream. "Countless" is almost literally true, for we were sailing through the famous Thousand Islands which threaten to choke the narrow stream, narrow enough here to be spanned by a bridge between Canada and the United States.

The Thousand Islands not only have given their name to a salad dressing, but are famous for their beauty, and it was easy for us to see why the maze of lush islands, big, little, and tiny, attracts tourists from far and near. It was just as easy to see why Bill Johnston was able to carry on a notorious career as "The Pirate of the Thousand Islands" in the early nineteenth century, prowling the waterways with a crew armed to the teeth in a swift six-oared longboat. Because he knew the maze of channels like the back of his hand, he could remain safely hidden, dashing out to capture passing boats, and swooping down Viking-like on peaceful Canadian farmers. In July 1838, accompanying her famous husband on government business, Lady Durham sailed through these channels and reported, "Our voyage by the Thousand Islands has been most prosperous, no appearance of

Pirate Johnston . . . steamboats . . . Fort Wellington . . .
Battle of the Windmill . . . Upper Canada Village . . . New France . . .
Samuel de Champlain . . . fur trade . . . timber . . . Jacques Cartier

---

Pirates or ill-disposed persons, but we heard afterwards that Bill Johnston, the most dreaded of these robbers, had been very near us."

Happily, as we sailed along under perfect conditions we saw no "ill-disposed persons". On the contrary, we met with hospitality and friendly waves wherever we went, especially in the Brockville Narrows, where we sailed through a parade of fifteen small, historic steamboats. This was a major event for Peter, who was excitedly certain that among them was his storybook favourite "Tootie the Tugboat". Penny, however, insisted that what we had spotted was "Scuffy", not "Tootie", and a fierce argument ensued.

Sailing along this placid stretch of river with the Canadian bank to port and the American shore always visible to starboard, we were constantly reminded that the river had been a no-man's-land between opposing British and American forces during the War of 1812, and at other times of tension. At Prescott we saw the outline of Fort Wellington overlooking the river and recalled the ruse played by its British occupants to surprise their Yankee foes entrenched in Ogdensburg. The story goes that the redcoats' midwinter armed drills on the ice in the centre of the river became such a boring routine that the Americans ignored it – until the day the troops came out for their drill and kept on going right across the ice, to capture the American outpost.

A mile and a half downriver from Prescott we passed the windmill that in November 1838 was the scene of, naturally enough, the Battle of the Windmill. This was a sad affair which, as one book put it, "would have been pure comic opera except for the fact that a few people actually got killed." Our old pirate friend Bill Johnston was involved, among roughly two hundred other ragtag Americans who landed in Canada and captured the windmill, but Johnston prudently decamped by night, and after four days of siege by the British and Canadian forces the Americans surrendered and their leader, Von Schoultz, was hanged.

Despite the fact that the original Canadian settlers along the entire riverbank were Loyalists fleeing in disapproval from the American Revolution, hostilities were the exception rather than the rule. In fact a healthy smuggling trade flourished across the river, as both groups of settlers refused to let laws get in the way of common sense. Much later, that same spirit of sensible co-operation produced the St. Lawrence Seaway, which was opened in 1959 by Queen Elizabeth II, Prime Minister John G. Diefenbaker, and President Dwight D. Eisenhower.

This gigantic feat of hydraulic engineering succeeded in opening up the river to huge seagoing ships, but it also helped our little fleet. The section after Prescott isn't called "the International Rapids Section" for nothing, but a series of locks have removed that problem and soon we were going through the Iroquois Lock, to the great excitement of Penny and Peter; a week before, they had read about how a lock is operated, and were desperate to pass on the news to anyone who would listen.

Summer in Ontario is very hot (a fact that astonishes those who think of Canada as a land of perpetual snow, where polar bears haunt the outskirts of every town). So we were glad of the cooling breezes that helped us along as we sailed down the river. Those fine summer conditions were providing us with a nice gentle introduction to the sterner stuff ahead, although with our smaller boat we had to put in longer hours than our companions to keep up with the fleet.

Into Lake St. Francis we sailed, to put in at Crysler Park, near the wonderful reconstruction of Upper Canada Village (where some historic buildings from the areas flooded out by the seaway have been preserved). It was odd to be sailing over drowned ghost towns, where streets and buildings lay deep below the

24

surface. At Cornwall we sailed under another bridge and knew that we had reached the northern tip of New York State. From now on the rich, flat plain of the St. Lawrence Lowland on either side would be Canadian territory.

Beyond Lake St. Francis we had left Ontario behind, and with Quebec on either bank were plunging into the heart of New France. The Beauharnois Canal carried us easily past the former rapids of Lachine and Les Cèdres. Here, in 1611, the redoubtable explorer Samuel de Champlain showed his mettle. Forty-four years old and totally unused to canoes, he chose to display his courage to the local Indian warriors by lashing himself to his canoe and setting off alone through the giant waves of the Lachine rapids. A few days before, two of three volunteers had drowned in a similar attempt. But Champlain made it through, as we did, to our berth at the hospitable Royal St. Lawrence Yacht Club.

At Lake St. Louis, of course, the Ottawa River flows in from the west. In novelist Hugh MacLennan's words, "It comes down broad and ale-coloured and joins the St. Lawrence, the two streams embrace the pan of Montreal Island, the Ottawa merges and loses itself, and the main stream moves north-eastward a thousand miles to the sea." We were bound for the sea, too, but it was impossible to pass the junction of the Ottawa without reflecting on that river's history. For this was the highway of the fur trade two hundred years ago, the route along which the fleets of canoes set out each spring loaded with trade goods that could end up in hide teepees in the Athabasca Country or in wooden longhouses beside the Pacific. Every fall these waters rang to the songs of voyageurs paddling triumphantly homeward, their canoes crammed with ninety-pound bales of fur that were bound for the warehouses of Montreal en route to Europe. It was the fur trade that made Canada, and its leaders were indeed the Caesars of the wilderness, their names still recalled in rivers like the Fraser and the Mackenzie, or in universities like McGill. And their Empire, of course, was called "the Empire of the St. Lawrence".

Even when European fashion changed and the fur trade

declined, the Ottawa continued its central role. For nineteenth-century Europe was building furiously and was hungry for timber. The Ottawa Valley was thickly forested with giant trees, and there were French Canadians and Irish, Scottish, and English settlers aplenty eager to spend their winters "hurling down the pine". So down these waters came the great squared-timber rafts, floating log booms with their custodians ensconced in huts in the middle, bound for the timber ships at Quebec.

We knew that in due course the world of history would fascinate our children as it fascinated us, and that they would be pleased by the idea of our tracing in reverse the first European voyage up the St. Lawrence by Jacques Cartier in 1535, in a ship not much larger than some in our fleet. But as we approached the bridges over the St. Lawrence at Montreal (the Champlain and Cartier bridges, of course), it wasn't the gigantic bridges or the glittering high-rises of the huge city beneath its mountain that excited them. It was the old Expo 67 site, with its fairground of Ferris wheels and roller coasters, that entranced them and held them wide-eyed.

Finally Penny breathed: "Mummy, are they there just for us?"

THE KIDS ADAPT

4

"**P**eter, get up here! Get up here!"

We had just spotted our first pod of beluga whales in the St. Lawrence, and Penny was beside herself with excitement. Peter, who is an avid animal-lover, lost no time in getting into the cockpit. The big white creatures were splashing alongside us not too far away and we could see three, four, five of them. And both children sat looking in the water long after the whales had disappeared.

"One came right up to the boat and took a biscuit from my hand," said Peter sleepily and imaginatively that night. "Mummy, I saw a hundred of them."

No matter that there were only a few for five minutes. Peter had seen something that perhaps few other children have the opportunity of enjoying. And that, of course, was one purpose of our trip – and an answer to all those who had worried about the children's education while we were roaming the high seas.

We had tried to prepared the children for their new life. Now the voyage itself, with all its new things to see and do, was reinforcing that preparation.

It was, of course, impossible to transfer to a 30-foot boat all the toys the children owned in a ten-room house. We took care to show the children the space they would have available for toys, and we had family discussions on how many and what sort of toys we should take with us.

"We should try to pick the ones you can do different things with," I suggested.

And I sighed with relief as Penny added, "Mummy, it's probably better to take small toys rather than big ones, isn't it?"

The children made their own first selection and were surprisingly intelligent about not trying to take everything they could, since all their toys had to fit into one large duffle bag each. There was, of course, no question that they had to have their very favourites with them. For Penny this was a falling-apart "Pooh Bear" and a handsome puppet beaver, given to her by her Auntie Helen. For Peter, it was a baby blanket which was in shreds and had a distinctive odour, together with Paddington Bear and Lambie Pie.

The toys they play with most have turned out to be their little Fisher-Price figures (and the cars they fit into), Lego (which has proved to be hard to find in many countries), and paper, pencils, crayons, and playing-cards.

As the trip progressed, I was surprised to find that they also played a lot with their stuffed animals. Partly, I think, this was because these animals became their companions in lieu of other kids, and partly because their new outdoor life attuned them more to the natural world.

Books have been extremely important. Reading aloud to the kids proved to be an enjoyable and educational cockpit activity. And while Peter and Penny were good listeners and liked almost any kind of book, the ones that really grabbed their attention were the books that had something to do with their new lifestyle. *The Children's Book of the Sea*, with its definitions of ports, harbours, locks, and how marine things work, was one of their favourites, and made the seven locks between Kingston and Montreal exciting events.

Penny's formal education would begin during our first year of voyaging, so I had a complete box of Grade 1 material from the Ontario Ministry of Education packed under her bunk. All provinces in Canada and states in the U.S. have their own requirements for correspondence education, and what they supply varies greatly. I must say that we were very pleased by the Ontario system. Penny's large box contained a complete package of thirty-nine weeks of study, together with rulers, crayons, pencils, and other material, all supplied at no cost. Her completed week's assignments were sent (whenever we reached port) to a teacher, who marked them and sent them back to our next port of call. Mrs. Kathryn Clare of Mississàuga never failed to include a sticker and some words of encouragement for her travelling pupil, personal feedback that was very important for our six-year-old. And the selection of books at her level (and beyond) that we brought along proved to be very valuable, too.

To teach Peter to read, I carefully packed Sidney Ledson's inestimable book *Teach Your Child to Read in 60 Days*, and found that it worked. At four, Peter was of junior kindergarten age, which meant that there were no formal textbooks for him – and there would be none for two years until he started Grade 1. So I brought along as many books as I could that had interesting pre-school materials such as joining dots, following mazes, and drawing and relating shapes. Peter really enjoyed all this material. Soon he regarded it as *his* homework, and could sit at the table for a couple of hours working away by himself.

Peter and Penny were both young enough that I was not too worried about replenishing their reading supply, though I knew this would be a problem farther down the line if we could not find children's books in English to purchase. As a partial solution I bought magazine subscriptions for both children. I chose two Canadian magazines that I thought would relate well to our voyaging, *Chickadee* for Peter and the more senior *Owl* for Penny. Both magazines are nature-oriented, with first-class information on animals, birds, and fish, together with excellent photographs, puzzles, stories, and projects. The postage on these was high, as I had the magazines forwarded to a friend in Toronto, who then airmailed them to us whenever she had a forwarding address. But it was well worth the cost, as the children looked forward to receiving *their own mail* whenever we were doing a pick-up. If more than one magazine arrived at a pick-up, I would let the kids have one issue in port, and save the second one for a sea crossing.

Sewing materials proved to be another useful item for both children. Penny could knit and had a large latch-hook project, while I had easy-to-do tapestry projects for both children. They both completed one tapestry project in the first six months, and I was glad to find another one for them when we got to Brazil. Spare needles and latch-hooks, incidentally, were very useful.

We had brought many materials and projects for the children, but their biggest toy turned out to be the boat itself. We estimate they spent about twenty-five per cent of their time with their more formal playthings, while the bulk of the day was spent in enjoying some aspect of the boat, which was their personal playground, just as it had been in our backyard. That the vessel now floated simply made it all the more interesting! And, because of the scale, it was relatively easy for us to keep an eye on them; after all, they were never more than thirty feet away!

If it was warm and sunny, the kids would be in the cockpit. The rule was they could play there without life-jackets if it was calm, but they had to wear them on demand, or if they wanted to move forward. If the weather was rough, as it was in the lower reaches of the St. Lawrence, we would put them in their safety harnesses. In really bad weather they stayed in the cockpit or below decks.

We soon discovered that if we folded the red cockpit canopy towards the stern, the kids would sit on the cockpit floor, making believe the canopy had provided them with a house, the floor of which was soon littered with toys and teasets.

On the day's long sail from Montreal to Trois-Rivières, the kids spent six hours below decks dressing up and making their own houseboat from the sheets and sleeping-bags that I had carelessly omitted to put away. They had no sooner draped things one way over the main cabin table than it was time to try another. It was easy to clear at day's end, and as far as I was concerned, it was a great activitiy that could be repeated as often as they liked.

When they moved forward on the bow, not only could they appreciate the vistas of the St. Lawrence and follow the progress of the other members of the fleet, but they could also make believe they were driving the boat themselves, which they often did, with proper exuberance. The rule when they were at the bow was that they had to sit down.

The race to spot the first freighter each day fired their competitive spirit, and it was a good game, because many large ships carry cargo up and down Canada's main waterway to the Atlantic Ocean. And then, as they began recognizing foreign flags, the children not only got a point for seeing a freighter, but got two points if they could identify its country of origin. In our first few weeks, we saw boats from France, Turkey, Panama, Russia, and Japan.

Penny also learned some of the rudiments of navigation. She has extremely sharp eyesight, and could read the buoy numbers before I could. We showed her the river charts and how to identify the buoys, and soon she was watching for them and then marking them off on the chart herself.

"Are these charts especially for children?" she asked one day. "Grown-ups don't need to have M for mud and R for rock, do they?"

And how did a working mother adapt to all this?

When I had first thought about the trip, I must admit I was worried about how I would adapt to spending twenty-four hours a day with the children – very different from only seeing them early in the morning and in the evening. Now I was quite astonished to find myself adapting as well as the kids! We were all in this new project together and were enjoying one another's company and the new challenges and adventures we were having each day. I found it interesting to watch Peter mastering a

32

new knot, though it might take him days to do it, or to see Penny trying to remember a new symbol on the chart. Their everyday learning was something I had never seen before.

Both kids were also eager to help whenever they could.

"Dad, can I help you with the sail?" or

"Can I kick the fenders overboard?" or

"Can I hold the rope?" was interesting and fun for them and (usually) helpful for us.

As for cooking, I have always been a proponent of an open kitchen – and nothing could have been more open than our galley, placed as it was between the children's bunks and about four feet away from the main salon. Cooking the evening meal became a total family affair, with the kids doing everything from peeling carrots to counting out the cutlery. Whenever I baked bread I wondered if we would ever get the dough into the pressure cooker as the kids pushed and pulled and kneaded away, flour flying freely down the companionway and into the cabin.

In my land-locked days, it was always a struggle for me to get out of bed at eight o'clock (Paul was always up first). On the St. Lawrence, however, our days started around 5 a.m. when Paul and I would be up and preparing to leave harbour. The kids, tired out with their new life and outdoor living, usually were dead to the world till about seven, sleeping through the alarm going off and one of the other captains knocking loudly on the hull to make sure we were awake. Then we'd be clumping around making the boat ready for sail and turning on the engine to head out of harbour, but even that didn't waken Peter or Penny.

It was nice to have the early-morning hours to ourselves. We could look at the charts for the day's sailing in peace, set up the cockpit, and enjoy a peaceful bowl of cereal. We might perhaps even get an hour's travel under our belts before two warm, huggable bodies hurled themselves into the cockpit demanding to be dressed, and eager for their usual breakfast of juice, cereal, and whole-wheat bread.

At the end of the day, when we reached the night's destination, shopping ashore became a treat for the kids, as it was such a contrast to being on the boat all day. For them, getting into port also meant racing around the other boats in our fleet to greet their new friends. Since Penny and Peter were the only youngsters in the group, our sailing companions were more than kind. They invited the kids on board, and kept an eye on them as they danced around the docks of that night's new and exciting port of call.

After a few days I asked the kids if they were missing school and day care and they both admitted to missing their young friends. But they then added that while they liked living ashore, like their parents they'd much rather be sailing.

ON TO
CAPE BRETON

5

T he St. Lawrence has been described as the main highway of New France. As we sailed downstream from Montreal towards Quebec City, it wasn't just the names of the towns we passed that showed their French origin, or the grand spires testifying to the devotion of each little riverside community. From *Lorcha*'s decks the land itself clearly showed its seigneurial origins, from the distant time when frontage on the river – the main means of transport – was essential. To this day, each thin strip of land runs at right angles to the river, as it has done for three centuries. In Hugh MacLennan's words, "Every inch of it is measured, and brooded over by notaries, and blessed by priests."

At Sorel we passed the mouth of the Richelieu, the traditional invasion route for Indian war parties raiding north or south. Like their canoes, the Indian route was adopted with enthusiasm by Champlain and his successors raiding south via Lake Champlain into the English colonies; New France's general, Montcalm, was the last to do so, repulsing an attack at Fort Ticonderoga in 1758. Naturally the English, and later the Americans, moved north along the same route, with Benedict Arnold making use of it to capture Montreal for the revolutionary forces in 1775. We saw no war parties, only a profusion of islands dotting the river between here and the mouth of the St. Francis, where the river branches into Lac St-Pierre.

Indian war parties . . . Captain James Cook . . . Quebec . . . Royal Mail vessel . . . stamp-collecting . . . Gaspé . . . Anne of Green Gables . . . the great cookie caper

We spent the night at the ancient north-shore town of Trois-Rivières, founded at Champlain's urging in 1634, and the mid-point on the old Chemin du Roi – the King's Highway – from Quebec City to Montreal. From that point on downstream the fresh-water flow of the river for the first time becomes affected by the ebb and flow of the tides. But we barely noticed as the sun continued to shine and the brisk, predominantly westerly winds seemed to be chasing us out of the Seaway.

As we followed our charts down toward the fortress of Quebec, we were entering the area charted by none other than Captain James Cook. His incredible voyages of exploration in the Pacific (which in a very small way we hoped some day to imitate) earned him a place in the annals of history. In 1757, however, with the ink scarcely dry on his master's warrant, Cook was sent to North America on the English warship *Pembroke* under Captain John Simcoe. England and France were fighting for the prize of North America (and the rich cod fisheries and inland fur trade that went with control of the continent), and had assembled the largest fleet ever seen in North America to do the job. No fewer than 150 vessels were assembled to take the fortress of Louisbourg on Cape Breton Island. Despite the fact that the French defences had absorbed so much money that Louis XV had complained to his Versailles courtiers that he expected to see the walls of Louisbourg appearing over the western horizon, the French fortress fell to an assault by land and sea, which left British forces free to move on to assault the key to New France, Quebec.

Seen from the river, the rock at Quebec – "the Gibraltar of North America" – is a daunting sight, a natural fortress looming up to dominate the river at its last narrow point. No wonder the French, like the Indians before them, made it their strong point, and no wonder the British forces, under General Wolfe and Admiral Saunders, had such a terrible time taking it in 1759. They had 200 ships, 13,500 sailors and marines, and 8,500 troops. In the end, after a long siege, it was English sea-power (and the charting skills of James Cooke) that allowed Saunders to slip part of his fleet upstream past the citadel, and then allowed Wolfe to make the famous night attack up the cliffs at the Anse au Foulon. The short, sharp battle next day on the Plains of Abraham outside the walls of the old city was indeed a "battle for a continent".

In the distant past, Quebec had a way of dealing briskly with invading fleets of English-speakers (fiery old Frontenac in 1689 rejected an English admiral's demand for surrender with the words "I have no reply other than from the mouths of my cannons"), but like other modern travellers we met with nothing but kindness, and the kids especially were thrilled by the old walled city. Here, in the provincial capital, "Admiral" David Ker received official greetings from the Premier of Quebec, for "Admiral" Ker's 36-foot *Thalia* had become a Royal Mail vessel for the trip, carrying official letters and greetings to the people of Newfoundland from the other Canadian provinces the fleet was to visit. The mail had to reach St. John's on August 3 for the newly issued stamps to be franked as first-day covers. This caught the imagination of the children, who were both stamp collectors from an early age. Peter, who had been soaking off stamps and putting them into albums since he was three, was especially excited.

"Mama, will be able to get some of those stamps?" he asked almost daily, at the same time worrying if the fleet was going to be able to deliver them in time or not.

Both Penny and Peter were to collect stamps from every new country they visited for the rest of the trip. They would spend hours trading with other boat children. Soon, if they saw any foreign flag on a yacht, they would row over and ask if the owner had any stamps to spare, which of course they always had. When we met new adults ashore, they would often say: "Oh, you must be the parents of the stamp collectors."

After Quebec City, the river widens steadily, the water is increasingly brackish, and the tides are high. With these new factors to consider, the planning and timing of passages becomes a bit more critical, and there were nightly convivial meetings of all the fleet captains to discuss plans for the following day. The fleet worked as a unit, but the different personalities of the individual boats inevitably emerged. If the skippers announced we would leave at 5 a.m. to catch the tide, we would hear the early birds starting their engines at 4 a.m. The more casual boats, by contrast, might not throw off their mooring lines until after seven. We always seemed to take a middle road and would usually be found somewhere in the centre of the fleet.

When the winds were favourable, the larger and better-crewed yachts took advantage by flying spinnakers, leaving some of the slower boats like us behind. But when we got to our destination, we never had to waste time asking where to tie up, as we could always spot the early arrivals.

And so on we swept, down the steadily widening river, with the rugged north shore disappearing in the distance. Round the Gaspé Peninsula we worked our way, reflecting on the courage of Jacques Cartier, who first discovered this "great river of Canada", sailing ever deeper into mystery. At Gaspé on July 24, 1534 (we anchored there on July 15, 449 years later!), he formally took possession of Canada on behalf of the French king, raising a wooden cross making the claim. The local Indian chief, incidentally, objected mightily; he didn't understand the cross or the strange shapes carved in it, but he knew what Cartier intended, for all of the French skipper's gestures of apology.

The current runs counter-clockwise around the Gulf of St. Lawrence, and as we hugged the southern shore it carried us comfortably around the Gaspé, past Chaleur Bay, and along the north shore of New Brunswick. Here many of the displaced

Acadians (familiar to everyone who has read *Evangeline*) finally found a home. Now, apart from the area around the mouth of the Miramichi, from Caraquet to Shediac the French language and the tricolour with the single star predominate in the fishing villages that dot the shoreline.

The fleet sailed on to Prince Edward Island to pick up another provincial message – and we marvelled at the fact that the fertile fields and the cliffs of this holiday paradise really are red, like the hair of the beautiful Island's most famous fictional heroine, Anne of Green Gables.

After Charlottetown we sailed east through Northumberland Strait. Now the Nova Scotia shore was to starboard, and we revelled not only in the scenery but in the rich crop of wonderful names that have sprung up along the coast. "Pugwash" reminded us of the philanthropist Cyrus Eaton. The story goes that another Eaton born in Pugwash emigrated to become a member of the United States Congress. There he was heckled by a questioner wondering "Where, may I ask, *is* Pugwash?" Eaton replied: "All the world knows that Pugwash is exactly halfway between Shinimicas and Tatamagouche!"

East from Tatamagouche near Caribou (where a ferry crosses to P.E.I.) lies the historic town of Pictou. The arrival there of the barque *Hector* in 1773 marked the start of a long immigration of Scottish Highlanders to Nova Scotia – a process, we like to think, that led to the eventual arrival of Fiona McCall in Toronto!

All of this was excellent sailing, but our luck had to change. The first time we were harbour-bound was just beyond Pictou, around Cape George. There, in the little fishing harbour of Ballentynes Cove, we spent two nights and a day, trapped by driving rain and high winds that sent spray shooting over the seawall.

The community is small, and two local women took pity on us, generously baking an enormous quantity of raisin scones and chocolate-chip cookies the evening before we were due to leave. They drove down the following morning at 8 a.m. to present us with the goodies – only to find we had all left, except for John Finney's *Clarissa II*. The two crew members, Nick Rucker and

40

Yves Galman, were only too delighted to accept this appetizing windfall on behalf of all the other yachts, and decided to have some fun.

Nick called Virginie Charpentier on *Genevieve II* on the vhf, our "party" line, to which everyone listened.

"Yves and I are going to try our hand at baking some cookies for everyone," he said. "Could you give us a couple of recipes – maybe raisin scones and, oh, chocolate-chip cookies?"

Virginie dutifully read out the recipes, answering such questions as:

"We don't have any of that . . ."

"Can we substitute this . . . ?"

"How many times that recipe to have enough cookies for the whole fleet?"

Soon everyone knew that Nick and Yves were baking cookies, and the disparaging comments about their abilities were flying thick and fast as we sailed through the Strait of Canso and under the causeway that links the Nova Scotia mainland with Cape Breton Island.

When the boats grouped together at the St. Peter's Port lock, Nick and Yves casually passed around their loaded trays of fabulous home-baked goodies.

"Do you really think they taste okay?" asked Nick anxiously, with a straight face. "Maybe I put in too many chocolate chips?" said Yves with a worried expression.

But the looks of astonishment on the rest of the fleet's faces as we bit into the glorious cookies were too much for them, and it was not long before they burst out laughing and shared the joke with us.

NEWFOUNDLAND
VIA FRANCE

6

We wound our way through the beauties of the Bras d'Or Lakes, the salt-water system that flows right to the centre of Cape Breton Island. The Scottish heritage is so strong here that Gaelic is still spoken in places, and we were not very surprised to find ourselves sailing through Barra Strait past Iona (with its reassembled Highland Village) in the direction of St. Andrews Channel. But we were bound for Baddeck, a charming holiday town on the spectacular Cabot Trail, but with more than one claim to fame. It was not only the birthplace of Hugh MacLennan, the eminent Canadian novelist and essayist whom we have quoted. It was also the summer home of Alexander Graham Bell, the inventor of the telephone and – as the extensive and fascinating museum here makes clear – of much else. Aircraft, hydrofoils, devices to help the deaf, Bell was deeply involved in all of them, and the excellent museum does full justice to a fascinating man.

We knew that we were going to need all the inventiveness we could muster, for after Baddeck the rehearsal was over. Now we were embarking on a 220-mile sail to Saint-Pierre and Miquelon, the French territorial islands off the south coast of Newfoundland. And we would be crossing the Cabot Strait, totally open to the whims of the Atlantic Ocean.

On this crossing we had a good navigation lesson.

We left Baddeck with a light following wind, which

Bras d'Or Lakes . . . Alexander Graham Bell . . . navigation lesson
. . . Miquelon . . . Saint-Pierre . . . Newfoundland fish . . .
"Newfy John" . . . fog . . . Cape Spear . . . St. John's welcome

turned to a headwind as we motored through the night. Then a southwest wind sprang up, building to a fresh breeze. We sailed with it, heading steadily eastward during a long, hard day. If all went well (and our navigation passed the test), we expected to see the lights on the south end of Miquelon at around midnight on our second night.

Soon after our DR ("Dead Reckoning" position, an estimation of the boat's position) showed us we should be sighting the lights, we began to see flashes far to the north of us. With the wind now about thirty knots, it was difficult to time the sequence of the lights, as they kept disappearing in the deep swells. We changed course northward to head for the distant flashes, only to find after a long couple of hours that it was the *north* Miquelon light. The south Miquelon light was not visible, though we should have been within its range.

Should we try to beat around the shallows of the south end of Miquelon in a strong and rising wind with high seas in the dark when the light was not visible? Or should we play safe and continue heading north, which would add an extra forty-five miles of sailing – and an extra day? We were cold and wet and tired, but we could rest up at Miquelon and sail to Saint-Pierre the following day.

"We'd better head for the harbour on the north end of Miquelon," I said to Fi. "It means we won't get much sleep tonight, but it's really a safer course."

It was a tough sail, with a mean beam wind all the way, and with the weather worsening the deeper we got into the bay at

43

the north end of the island. It was a weary crew who tied up at 0430.

Three hours later the skipper of the fishing boat we had tied to rapped on the hull to say he was leaving, so we would have to shift to another dock.

"Oh well," I said philosophically. "Now we're up, let's go into the village and get some croissants and fresh bread."

It was scarcely nine o'clock when we walked into the boulangerie.

"Du pain?" said the baker in astonishment. "C'est fini! I saw you come in at four-thirty – you should have walked in for bread then. We bake early here!"

Breadless, we left for Saint-Pierre, twenty-five miles distant, heading into the still-fresh southwest wind to rendezvous with the rest of the fleet. It was a tough sail, but we knew that we could rely on our charts. Before the islands were handed back to France, as a sort of consolation prize at the end of the Seven Years War, the British Admiralty had James Cook accurately chart these waters before the peace treaty was signed in 1763.

The entrance to Saint-Pierre harbour is from the northeast, and with the wind blowing right on our nose, we made our way, with a tip of the hat to Captain Cook, through the off-lying islets. In the open sea, it was blowing thirty knots, but in the harbour entrance it was over forty as the wind rushed down the cliff face and tossed us about.

We were glad to finally raft alongside Don and Lyn Cash's *Sixpence*, and expected a warm welcome and congratulations from all of our friends. Instead, we were immediately surrounded by irate skippers.

"Where the hell have you been?" roared Ed Pursey.

"Why didn't you answer our calls?" Keith Burley wanted to know.

"Why are you so late?" demanded John Smith of *Turning Point*.

We had spoken to Ed Pursey about twenty hours earlier on the vhf, and since at that point we were several hours ahead of him, we had been "expected" in Saint-Pierre fifteen hours earlier. When Ed tied up and several hours had passed without our arrival, the boats began calling us on the vhf. But Saint-Pierre is a tall rock, with its mass directly between its harbour and Miquelon. We never heard the calls. After several hours, the fleet notified the Newfoundland and Nova Scotia Coast Guard that we were overdue.

To be told we were posted overdue and missing gave me an eerie feeling. All too often those words apply to boats later found wrecked on some isolated coast or lost at sea, things I can't bear to imagine happening to my small boat and family. We called the Coast Guard to let them know we were not lost, and promised the rest of the fleet that we would call on the radio if we ever deviated from a planned stop again.

Our next sail was an ambitious one, two hundred miles around the rugged Avalon Peninsula that forms the southeastern tip of Newfoundland – and of Canada. Newfoundland (accent on the last syllable, please) was England's first colony, and the last province to join Canada in 1949 after a hard-fought referendum. But these hardy folk – a mixture of Irish and West Country English, with a heady dash of Scots, French, Portuguese, and Basque thrown into the brew – didn't lose their delightful distinctiveness. There's the famous story that shortly after the province joined Canada, a federal fisheries officer sailed up to challenge a Newfoundlander for fishing without a licence.

"They's Newfoundland fish!" protested the islander.

"How can you tell them from mainland fish?"

The reply was unanswerable. "Oh, I throws back the ones with the big mouths!"

As we rounded Cape Race at the base of the Avalon Peninsula we were in the oldest fishing territory in the New World. It was the unbelievable richness of the cod stocks (so thick in the water that they impeded the passage of his ship, according to one early explorer) that brought bold fishermen from Western Europe to this oceanic gold rush. The Portuguese and the French were the first, followed by the Basques in the 1520s, then by the English. Fifty years later, nearly four hundred ships made the voyage each summer, which meant that more ships and men were involved in the supposedly prosaic business of cod-fishing off Newfoundland and drying the fish at temporary stations ashore than in the entire romantic Spanish trade with the Caribbean, Mexico, and Peru. While European settlement languished elsewhere in North America, by 1611 some ten thousand men used Newfoundland as a base for the greatest fishing enterprise ever.

It was cod fishermen who gave the world the idea of "Red Indians", since the Beothuks in Newfoundland painted their bodies with ochre. It was these same fishermen who provided the labour force that made Newfoundland the great pirate centre of the early seventeenth century. Pirate captains like Peter Easton and Henry Mainwarring ruled the free port of St. John's from their fortress in nearby Harbour Grace, planning raids on the Spanish colonies far to the south.

Three hundred years later, St. John's Harbour played an even more important role in a greater cause. For here – under the naval name of "Newfy John" – the great Second World War convoys assembled before running the U-boat gauntlet to bring supplies to Britain. Thousands of men – in troopships, in merchant ships loaded with arms, ammunition, and desperately needed food, and in the gallant corvettes that performed the escort role of sheepdog – sailed out of St. John's never to return. But the survivors never forgot the hospitality of the people of St. John's. One of them, James B. Lamb, the author of *The Corvette Navy* and *On the Triangle Run*, remembers being invited off the street to dinner by a St. John's schoolteacher, who then wrote to him until his death.

Before we got a chance to taste that hospitality, we assembled at our staging-area in Bay Bulls, where our fleet and the welcoming Newfoundland yachts got together to organize our arrival en masse at St. John's. So far, so good. But the short 22-mile sail from Bay Bulls to St. John's – despite the excellent charts based on the work of our old friend James Cook, who mapped all of Newfoundland's 2,000-mile coastline – was to throw a new challenge at us. Fog – and fog as only a Newfoundlander can understand the term: fog thick enough to shovel.

46

As soon as we saw the dense bank up ahead, we decided to stay close to one of the boats with Loran, an accurate electronic navigational device, so we motored about three boat-lengths off the port quarter of *BetPamBek*, with the masthead of *Thalia* in view just ahead. The fog suddenly thickened, however, and the boats ahead were lost to view. I increased my speed and cut over (I thought) to where they should be, but suddenly we were quite alone. All the other boats had been swallowed up.

BetPamBek began sounding her foghorn and Penny started blowing ours. Soon foghorns boomed all over the place. We couldn't see one another, but at least it sounded like a staging-area, and after about twenty minutes we were able to close ranks and motor along at four knots, keeping only a boat-length apart.

As we neared Cape Spear, the fog at last began to clear and more vessels appeared out of the gloom. With *Thalia* leading the way, and the rest of the fleet making a chevron formation, we sailed triumphantly around the Cape and into our final harbour, the ghosts of those earlier explorers, fishermen, pirates, and weary convoy escorts sailing right beside us.

And what a welcome! The lighthouse and its pathway were lined with Newfoundlanders, the crowds on Marconi's famous Signal Hill were a forest of enthusiastically waving arms, and the old cannons were firing welcoming volleys – of blanks. Car horns mixed with boat horns, ship's bells and whistles, and the ever-present fog signals to make a joyful cacophony as we passed through the Narrows, the entrance to St. John's Harbour, where we saw at last the hill where Sir Humphrey Gilbert ceremoniously took possession of Newfoundland in the name of Queen Elizabeth on August 5, 1583 – exactly four hundred years before.

Once inside the harbour, we skirted the city-side breakwall to salute the cheering crowds, estimated at twenty thousand, but sounding like five times that number. Penny and Peter were wild with excitement and they waved and cheered madly from *Lorcha*'s bow. It was hard for them to believe that this tremendous welcome was for us. Suddenly I noticed, however, that Peter wasn't looking quite as cheerful as he had been. In fact, he seemed downright worried.

47

"What's the matter, Pete?" I asked. "Is all that noise bothering you, or what?"

"It's an awful lot of people meeting us," he said, and paused. "I'm just a bit worried that if they all want some of those stamps, there won't be any for us!"

"Don't worry," I said gently. "I think everyone who made the journey will be able to get some of those stamps if they want them. Especially a collector like you."

It was a wonderful climax to our journey, but it was also the last time the nine boats who had made it to St. John's would be together. Three of the vessels would be left for the winter in either Newfoundland or Nova Scotia. John Smith was headed for Florida. *Thalia, BetPamBek, Genevieve II*, and *Clarissa II* would be returning to Lake Ontario via New York and the Erie Canal. And we on *Lorcha* were already preparing for our first ocean crossing, the 1,100-mile trip to the mid-Atlantic islands of the Azores.

THE FIRST OCEAN CROSSING

7

"**T**his is the passenger liner *Queen Elizabeth II* calling the yacht *Lorcha*. *Queen Elizabeth II* calling the yacht *Lorcha*."

Paul and I looked at each other in astonishment, then stood up in the cockpit to scan the horizon. We were on the second day of our first ocean crossing, sailing out of St. John's, to the Azores, 1,100 miles southeast.

How could the *Q.E. II* know about us? Could she see us? And why was she calling? Was she inviting us over for a cocktail, a shower, or dinner? Had she perhaps heard of *Lorcha* through the *Toronto Star*, who were carrying weekly stories on our voyaging? Did she want to borrow half a dozen eggs?

When you're on your first ocean crossing, life is so full of first experiences that your mind races all over the place as you deal with each one. Right now, I was concentrating on working our new VHF equipment. It's really very simple, but we found ourselves whispering to each other.

"You get it."

"No, you answer it."

Taking a deep breath, I picked up the unfamiliar microphone.

"Yacht *Lorcha* standing by. Over."

The liner's next comment was even more astonishing.

"This is the *Queen Elizabeth II* now returning your call. How can we help you?"

Call from the Queen Elizabeth II *. . . the VHF . . . freighter fixation*
. . . seasickness . . . keeping watch . . . self-steering . . . Azores High
. . . trailing log . . . gale warning . . . rogue wave . . . cockpit showers
. . . another yacht . . . land ho!

Paul and I looked at each other in astonishment and I could feel an incredible urge to giggle coming over me.

"We haven't called you," I said carefully, holding the white microphone close to my mouth and pressing the transmitting button. "We don't need any help. We can't even see you on the horizon. Over."

Just then another voice broke in. It was beginning to feel like Piccadilly Circus instead of the middle of the ocean.

"Mais non," said a French voice. "This is a *French* yacht calling the *Queen Elizabeth*. Come in, please."

Our first trans-Atlantic crossing introduced us to the use of the VHF radio, a parting present from my workmates in Toronto. It was turning out to be a wonderful gift, all the more appreciated because it wasn't planned in our original budget. Now we wouldn't be without one. It's an important safety factor, providing us with vital information from passing ships. It's also fun. Out on the ocean, the VHF is the local open switchboard.

"Hello, large freighter on our starboard quarter. Hello, large freighter on our starboard quarter. This is the Canadian yacht *Lorcha*. Come in, please."

We don't call every vessel we see, but it's a good way of letting the larger ships know you are around. We found that ninety-nine per cent of the ships we spoke with were more than willing to pass on the exact Greenwich Mean Time and the latest weather information, and to give us a position. In fact, the custom of getting exact latitude and longitude from a freighter has coined a new phrase among yachties: "freighter fixation"! Not to be relied on to

51

get one across an ocean, of course, but very acceptable as a position check nevertheless.

Our call from the *Queen Elizabeth* had come about because we had spoken with a St. John's fishing trawler only a couple of hours before. A trawler, by the way, whose captain had broken into peals of laughter when he heard that we were going to the Azores. He was only about a quarter of a mile from *Lorcha* when he called us, so he could see the yacht clearly. "You're not going across the Atlantic in that little boat," he said incredulously. And a great roar of laughter followed.

As for us, we were on our second day out of St. John's and none of us was feeling much like laughing. We had always been such steadfast travellers that the thought of seasickness had never entered our minds. But the bucking, confused seas caused by 20- to 30-knot winds over the shallow Grand Banks had affected the whole family. Both kids were vomiting, and Paul and I were unable to eat or drink. The family's total consumption in two days had been three slices of bread with honey – divided among all four of us. To my chagrin, I couldn't find the Gravol suppositories I had brought for the children (just in case), though I did have some children's seasickness tablets. I got Penny to swallow one, but little Peter just couldn't manage it.

That night we again all stayed in our day clothes – Peter and Penny sleeping in the big double bunk for comfort instead of their own berths, with Paul and I, as usual, taking turns on watch and sleeping in the starboard berth when not at the helm.

The question of keeping watch seems to be a hot issue among yachtsmen. Everyone keeps a 24-hour watch near shore and in the shipping lanes, of course, but many boats opt not to keep watch when they're in mid-ocean. Some boats prefer to keep a partial watch, with an alarm waking someone up every fifteen or thirty minutes. That person then pops up to have a quick look round the horizon.

We keep watch twenty-four hours, as we just feel it's safer that way. In our first six months of travel, we called no fewer than three freighters during the night to tell them they were on a collision course with us.

We also find that after a few days our bodies adjust so well to the broken-sleep routine that the pattern that's established is almost comfortable. It is only the first few days that are tiring. We find it most comfortable to keep two-hour watches during the day, and three-hour watches at night, and since we've found that certain hours suit each of us best, we keep the same watches. Paul always takes the first three-hour, watch from 10 p.m. to 1 a.m., and I'm always on from 1 to 4 a.m. Paul always sees the sun rise, and I'm in the cockpit when the kids wake up.

But by the third day, getting used to our watch routines was the least of our problems, for Peter and Penny were both very sick indeed. Peter was vomiting every hour on the hour, and we had to do something. I decided to use my tablet Gravol as a suppository, and even though Peter was extremely upset at the idea ("Mummy, please don't do it"), I inserted tablets in both children.

As no one was eating much and it looked as though Paul would still be feasting on one quarter-slice of bread for lunch and another quarter for dinner, I went through all the fresh food to see how it was faring. We don't carry ice, so most of it, alas, had to be thrown overboard. Over went the fresh fish fillets we had cut the morning before we left St. John's, away went the cucumbers, the lettuce, the mung beans, and the Newfoundland bake-apples, all food that we had planned to eat in a couple of days.

Everyone was washing out his or her mouth every two hours to try to keep some liquid in the body, and Paul was the only one who could even sip a little water.

But day three did have its good points. We had never used the self-steering gear thus far, as the weather and our general malaise had not been conducive to Paul's experimenting with it, so we had been hand-steering all the way, which, of course, had only added to our exhaustion. But with the seas abating slightly and Paul feeling better, he was able to set the Hydrovane for four hours in the afternoon. What a magic piece of equipment. The red wind-vane wagged to and fro as *Lorcha* slid over each wave. Paul sat in the cockpit with nothing to do but watch in fascination as our indefatigable helmsman brought *Lorcha* back on course whenever a wave pushed her head around. It was a wonderful reprieve, even though the wind quietened down so much in the evening that we had to turn the engine on and go back to handling the helm manually.

By evening, although the seas remained rough, the kids were much better. They were still not able to eat, but neither of them was vomiting any more and Peter sipped at a spoonful of water. As they were obviously much weaker than when they started, I wanted them to stay in their relatively stable condition and decided to keep them on the Gravol tablet suppositories every eight hours.

On day four we got two position checks from passing freighters, including one from the Polish freighter *Dadouch Kokushka*, which was quite literally on a collision course with us, travelling west to east. We were very glad that we were able to call her and inform her that we were altering course. By the silence at the other end and the ten minutes it took for her to call us back, it was fairly obvious she hadn't seen us. We got a very accurate position from this ship!

It was 6 a.m. and still dark when I spotted her, and Penny had woken up when we were talking. Later I heard her explaining the situation to Peter.

"Don't worry, Peter. Mummy says we might be going to bump a freighter, but it won't be hard. And they're going to try not to."

That evening we had our first light meal in four days. I'm almost ashamed to reveal what it was – a small packet of instant macaroni and cheese, followed by a two-person mix of instant chocolate pudding. It was more than enough for the four of us, and as soon as I had eaten a couple of mouthfuls I could feel my face getting flushed and hot with the energy intake. For the children it was perfect.

"Mummy, that was a wonderful supper," said Penny, very impressed. "This is the best day we've had."

We were now at a turning-point in our voyage. We were off the Grand Banks, though we still had not reached the Azores mid-Atlantic High, the area of high pressure that would mean warm west winds and sunny sailing. There was still an ocean swell, but in the deeper waters we no longer had the rough, confused seas that were making us all sick.

Paul was getting more and more expert with the self-steering gear, which was now working for most of the day, giving us a welcome break. The food was shooting energy back into our bodies, and for the first time in four days I felt well enough to change my clothes and get the children into pyjamas. We were all now sipping a little water. By day five, the kids were off the Gravol and I made scrambled eggs for breakfast. Never had eggs tasted so good.

We had, of course, been keeping a dead-reckoning position, estimating our position from our compass course, and from the distance run through the water recorded on our trailing log. A trailing log is a purely mechanical aid, needing no power, which consists of a thirty-foot-long piece of light line with a weighted spinner on the end which is towed behind the boat. A dial on deck records the distance travelled through the water. That morning Paul was well enough to do his first celestial sights. The moon and the sun were both up, so he was able to get a position without waiting for an afternoon sight. Our dead-reckoning and sextant sights were within ten miles of each other. Pretty good!

Another factor contributing to our well-being was the warmer temperature. Over the Grand Banks we had been wearing ski underwear, hats, and mitts, but we were now able to shed most of our outer garments. And despite the fact that the boat was fairly heeled over and I had to sit on the galley floor to mix the dough, I was able to bake some fresh bread and let it rise in the sun.

It was a terrific day for the kids, who were infused with energy and held an ambitious toy festival below decks. I think they had every toy they owned strewn around the main cabin, but I didn't mind a bit, as it was such a relief to see them happy and feeling better. "Hey, ocean sailing's not so bad," I remember thinking to myself.

We got two freighter fixes that night. The *Hoegh Falcon*, carrying crude oil from Norway to Quebec, told us there were two days of good weather ahead. But a scant four hours later the Dutch vessel *Ned Lloyd*, making for the Gulf of Arabia, had disturbing news.

"The winds are going to head you for the next two days. And the Azores High has moved four hundred miles southeast," the radio officer told us; he suggested we turn south to pick up the westerlies that were around latitude 40°N.

Indeed, the winds were heading us and getting stronger. Soon we had no choice but to sail south and were, in fact, almost sailing away from our destination, on a course of 240 degrees instead of 140 degrees.

Bash. Bash. Crash. Crash. The waves breaking over the bow were washing under the canvas forehatch cover, forcing water into the forecabin. Paul went below to stuff the inside of the hatch with rags and that seemed to solve the problem. We were relieved to find from our mid-Atlantic test that otherwise the boat was watertight.

We were now reefed three panels, and the only consolation to the worsening weather was our delight in the self-steering gear. It was now working twenty-four hours a day and was handling the heavy winds and the fifteen-foot waves with power and assurance. We were able to spend our watches sitting snugly under the lee side of the canvas dodger – safe, dry, and able to rest and relax instead of fighting with the heavy helm.

With the weather worsening, Paul checked all the foredeck lashings. This was a wise precaution, because during his watch, the wind blew a moderate gale at force 8, with gusts to force 9. The waves hurled themselves at the hull with such force that you would literally flinch at the sound – and then there was the bang as the boat slid over the top of a wave to drop into the trough. The motion was relentless. On and on. All night the noise was terrible, and neither of us was able to relax on our off-watches, though the kids slept right through the night.

When I stood up to scan the horizon, I had to hang on to the dodger to prevent myself from being hurled onto the cockpit floor. And I had to bob up and down, ducking and weaving like a boxer, to avoid the stinging spray that was whipped off the

56

The Newfoundland flag flies behind as Penny and Peter "steer" *Lorcha* down the St. Lawrence Seaway.

Penny watches the rest of the Ontario fleet crowd into the Eisenhower lock.

It's time to check the chart in Baddeck, Nova Scotia, before heading for Newfoundland. Making plans are David Ker of *Thalia* (Admiral of the fleet), Don Cash of *Sixpence*; Jim Midwinter of *Esmeralda* (and later the Canadian Embassy in Venezuela); Paul, and David Anderson of *Folie*.

On the passage from Newfoundland to the Azores, *Lorcha* had to contend with high seas. Sometimes the tiller was lashed (above); sometimes a young steersman got into the act.

The sail is reefed down to two panels and the North Atlantic swells are as cold as usual, but Penny and Peter obviously feel right at home.

In the Azores it was sobering to see a sperm whale, hunted the traditional way, being cut up at the whaling factory in Pico.

Ashore in mountainous Madeira Paul and the children enjoy their 6-kilometre ride downhill in a local wicker sled.

Coming ashore in Las Palmas in the Canary Islands is not always easy at low tide, even for the younger members of the family. Nor is climbing the steep mountains of Tenerife easy, but here Penny and Peter enjoy the company of Sandi Van Herk from the Canadian yacht *Eryngo*.

After finding the last Master Weaver in the Cape Verde Islands far up an isolated mountain on the island of São Tiago, Paul and Fiona are welcomed by Damasio Mendes Tuaures and his wife.

A friendly Cape Verdean woman in the market town of Santa Catalina tries to sell some of her "panos".

Crossing the South Atlantic to Brazil there's nothing to beat a bracing
shower bath in the cockpit.

foaming white wave tops to fly from the bow right past the dodger, over which I was trying to peer.

At dawn we had another surprise. Just as we were changing watches, there was a mighty roar, and a white express train hit the hull, almost turning the boat around before disappearing into the darkness. We had experienced our first rogue wave – the single wave that for some reason is nearly twice the height of the "normal" storm wave and often charges across the ocean in a different direction from the other waves. If it had hit the boat beam on, we would have been knocked down, and heaven only knows what might have happened. But when it struck, there was no time for fear or reaction. One minute it was there, and the next – gone. But its tremendous force flattened the sea, and an hour later the depression had blown itself out, leaving an eight-foot swell that now seemed tame.

By afternoon the weather was so pleasant that a school of dolphins dropped by to tell us we had at last reached the Azores High and could expect some pretty nice sailing. And indeed the sun poured energy back into us even though we were tired from having been up most of the night, and a refreshing shower seemed just the right idea. Paul got out our black plastic water bag and let it heat in the sun. We hung it overhead from the boom and then everyone took turns standing underneath to get a fresh-water rinse and soap-down. It was heaven to get the salt out of one's hair, and the children had so much squealing fun that they could have been under a sprinkler in some Toronto park. Later, they were delighted to find a small flying fish on deck, and they examined it in minute detail.

Days eight and nine were perfect sailing days. We set our course and just sailed and sailed at a constant five knots with the wind aft of beam. This is what I had always dreamed ocean sailing was like! I took time out to check all the fresh vegetables, putting aside for immediate use anything bruised or with a tiny spot of rot on it, and I also turned the eggs to keep them fresh.

On day ten we spoke to the passing British tanker *Maxwell Clarke*. We asked her for a position, but she requested our dead-reckoning one first.

"Oh, jolly good," said the radio officer when he heard it. "I'm glad to get confirmation. That's close to our position – we're using celestial and dead reckoning, too!"

This 10,000-ton oil tanker had no satellite navigation, either!

We were now only a day away from the westernmost island of Flores in the Azores, and for some reason I asked Paul to leave the VHF on all night. At midnight we heard the strangest call of all – another yacht chatting with a freighter. We couldn't see the lights of either vessel, but they had to be fairly close for us to be able to pick up their conversation, and I could hardly wait for the transmission to end to try to contact the yacht ourselves.

"Hello, yacht crossing the Atlantic and in range of the Azores. This is the Canadian yacht *Lorcha*, approximately twenty-four hours west of Flores. Come in, please."

Fritz Warren, the former Mayor of Sausalito and now captain of the 41-foot Californian ketch *Truly Fair*, came on the air.

"Hello, yacht *Lorcha*," he called. "This is incredible. Give us your exact position."

We worked out that *Truly Fair* was about twenty miles behind us and learned that she had been at sea for twenty-one days, out of Cape May, New Jersey. We arranged to leave our VHFs on so we could talk with each other – and to rendezvous in the small harbour of Santa Cruz on the east side of Flores.

Making your first landfall after an ocean crossing is an exciting moment, and we were glad to have someone to call after eagle-eyed Paul had spotted the dim outline of the small island on the horizon.

But our adventure was not quite over. We found the picturesque town of Santa Cruz on the hillside easily enough, but it was completely surrounded by jagged volcanic rock and the waves were pounding on a lee shore. We made a few passes until we spotted someone onshore, apparently gesturing to what looked as though it might be a thirty-foot gap in the rocks. Paul examined the extrance with the binoculars.

"It's pretty narrow," he said. "But I think we can go through, and there seems to be clear water to starboard."

58

We took the boat through, slowing down as much as we could in the heavy seas, and found ourselves in a tiny harbour. It was impossible to tie alongside, as the surging groundswell was at least three feet, but we got close enough to the quay for Carlos Manes, a local fisherman, to jump on board and help us locate the mooring buoy and chain. Even that was not sufficient to hold the boat, and Paul worked busily getting additional lines ashore. I radioed *Truly Fair*, now visible outside the harbour, to stand by until we were secure.

By now the whole village had come down to watch the two yachts come in, and a boat went out to guide *Truly Fair* in and to help settle her with two anchors and four lines ashore. We were too tired to go visiting and it was too rough to land ashore, so, waving happily at our new, but now close, trans-Atlantic friends, we promised to get together as soon as we had all had a few hours' sleep.

We lay down and closed our eyes, secure in the warm knowledge that we and the children had come through testing conditions and safely made our first ocean crossing.

IN THE AZORES

8

"At Flores in the Azores, Sir Richard Grenville lay." That's the opening line of Tennyson's poem about the *Revenge*, the gallant English ship that took on over fifty Spanish galleons in a famous, though doomed, fight. But we were much more interested in another fight from the same era, for all the way from Newfoundland we had been sailing on the path taken by Peter Easton in 1614 on his most famous piratical raid, perhaps the biggest hold-up of all time.

Each year the Spanish conquerors of the New World sent all of the year's production of gold and silver back home, assembled in one great convoy called the Plate Fleet. Its assembly and route were a heavily guarded secret, but word reached Easton in Newfoundland that the Spanish Plate Fleet would soon be leaving the West Indies bound for the Azores. Easton set sail (on our route) with fourteen ships, and set an ambush south and west of the islands. The Spanish fleet lumbered right into the trap and the great Easton made off with four Spanish ships containing that year's entire treasure from Central America.

That was one of the most dramatic incidents in the history of the Azores, or, to use the proper Portuguese term, the "Arquipelago dos Açores". Although the date of the archipelago's discovery is a matter of dispute (claims range from 1317 all the way to 1427), what is without dispute is that the Azores have always played

Spanish Plate Fleet . . . island of flowers . . . engine problems . . .
hove to . . . fouled propeller . . . morning swim . . . Faial Allied base
. . . Sea Week . . . Café Sport . . . cruising greats . . . charging bull
. . . José Dimas . . . whaling station . . . prison toys

---

an important part in Portuguese history. They played a role in the conquest and defence of the Portuguese strongholds on the coast of North Africa; later, they were a port of call for the caravels on their way to and from India and the Spice Islands; and, of course, they gave vital support to the expeditions off to explore the New World.

There are nine good reasons to visit these mid-Atlantic islands, and the reasons are named Flores, Corvo, Faial, Pico, Graciosa, Terceira, São Jorge, São Miguel, and Santa Maria. On this visit we spent five weeks in the island group, visiting four of the islands. We liked them all, and plan on returning some day to visit the others.

All of the islands are of volcanic origin – some claim that this was the site of the legendary city of Atlantis – and you'll see hundreds of dramatic and contrasting extinct volcanoes. Their harsh outlines stand in vivid contrast to the islands' natural fauna and flora – and nowhere was the contrast sharper than in our first port of call, the second-smallest and the westernmost island, Flores, the island of flowers.

Imagine hedges of blue and pink hydrangeas dissecting the small green fields and cascading over the narrow roadways, while hibiscus, cannas, azaleas, and camellias grow in careless and glorious profusion. Everywhere.

Our time in Flores was spent wandering around the lush surrounding countryside, eating a superb three-course lunch every day at the one local restaurant for almost nothing, watching the fishermen launch or pull up their boats to land the day's catch, or walking along the rocky beach to swim in one of the natural rock pools.

It's hard to imagine anyone giving up the chance to stop here. But that's just what Joshua Slocum, out of Yarmouth, Nova Scotia, did on his epic single-handed voyage around the world in 1895. Slocum was not attracted by the floral beauty ashore and sailed on to make Faial his first port of call. We decided to make Faial our second stop.

We left Flores early in the morning with the sun shining and a favourable wind. For a few hours we were in the company of our old friend *Truly Fair* of Sausalito, California. We chatted on the VHF, basked in the sun, and Fi baked a fresh loaf for lunch as we watched the bigger boat pull away. It was only 135 miles to Faial and *Truly Fair* expected to be in harbour early the next morning, while we were hoping to make it by lunch-time.

But forty hours later it was pitch black and we were hove to about twenty miles off Faial in a rough sea. It was raining hard, with a 25-knot wind heading us and a strong foul current against us. In these conditions, we usually motorsail to windward. Now, however, the plumbing on our diesel tank was giving us problems; it was leaking air, and though I continued to bleed the lines, five minutes later the engine would stall again. With the engine out of the picture, we were making no progress, so at midnight we hove to. We needed to get some rest and to rethink our problem. As the shore lights receded into the distance we could see that we were being swept further and further from the island.

At about 2 a.m., I realized how I could get the engine working again.

"Wake up, Penny," I whispered. "I want you to move to my bunk –I need to get under yours."

With Penny asleep again in minutes and Fiona watching, I lashed a jerry can to Penny's quarterberth. I then rigged a siphon hose from the can directly to the fuel pump, to bypass the plumbing problem. With the engine box open it would be noisy and, though I jammed rags in and taped up the hose at the mouth of the jerry can, the rough seas meant that we would also slop fuel around. But I was sure the engine would run.

At that moment I gashed my thumb on some sharp engine point, and it started to bleed too badly for me to continue. So Fiona bound me up as I sat and contemplated my new system. It was not long before I was able to switch on the motor and hear the engine running sweetly.

"Well done," said Fiona enthusiastically. "Let's go."

Smiling proudly, I put the engine in gear.

"CLunk. Clunk. CLUNK."

I switched off the engine as quickly as I could, my heart sinking. I knew at once what had happened. In my fatigue and distress, I had forgotten to pull in our trailing log line. With the boat hove to, the loose line had worked its way under the hull and now the line, weight, and spinner were wrapped around the propeller.

We consider ourselves cautious and safety-conscious sailors. I have been sailing for twenty years now, and just when I think I've made every seagoing error possible, another comes up to humble me.

"I'm afraid you'll have to swim for it, sweetheart, to get under the boat to free the propeller," I said apologetically. "I don't think we can get to harbour without using the engine."

Fiona is a much better swimmer than I, so is usually assigned to the underwater jobs. The water was also very cold, and anyone going overboard might not, because of hypothermia, be able to climb back on again. It thus made sense that the stronger person stay on board. I could pull Fiona back on, but she might not be able to get me back on board if I were in difficulties.

We waited until dawn, for it would be doubly dangerous to swim around in the dark. But we wanted to get the job done before the children awoke. At first light, Fiona, with ski-underwear, socks, and toque as well as a safety harness and lifeline, went over the side. I was equally warmly dressed, and I too had on my safety harness and lifeline. As Fiona slowly descended into the water (with many vivid descriptions of how cold it was), I hung over the side with my knife ready.

The boat rose and fell with each passing wave, making it very dangerous for Fiona to get underneath the hull in case she was struck on the head as the stern dropped. The water was so cold that she did not want to get completely immersed. She held on to the boarding-ladder and probed with her foot.

"I'll have to take my socks off," she gasped. "I can't get enough purchase with them on."

She peeled them off as quickly as she could, and found that though the line was wrapped around the prop, the sinker and the spanner were hanging free.

"I think I can get hold of them okay," she said, and her head disappeared. She soon reappeared with something in her hands below the water. Wrapping my legs around the pushpit, I hung head first as far as I could over the side and, with my head now bobbing in the waves – it *was* cold – cut the line as close to the prop as I could.

"That will probably do it," I gasped, trying to heave myself back on board, using Fiona to get some purchase. I was soon safely back and then had to pull Fiona in. She had only been in the water for a few minutes, but her teeth were chattering fiercely and she had little strength left when I managed to roll her up on deck.

We both stripped off our clothes in the cockpit and I wrapped Fiona up in dry towels just as the children were waking.

"Were you swimming, Mama?" asked Penny in an aggrieved voice. "Why didn't you wait for me?"

But she soon sensed that all was not well and cuddled up to Fiona, helping her to warm up.

But the engine ran well on my jury-rigged tank, giving no further problems, and though there was still some line wrapped around the prop, it didn't hinder our progress. Several hours later we chugged into Faial harbour.

Although Faial was discovered by Diego Silves of Portugal in 1427, Flemish explorers were the earliest settlers, first arriving on the island in 1468 under the leadership of Jos van Hurtere, whose name lives on in the island's main town of Horta. It was easy to spot the strong continuing Flemish influence in the many windmills, still lazily turning in the wind to grind maize for the local specialty, cornbread. Not much seems to have changed since their early installation, and the mill we visited ground the corn at the rate of about a cup a minute.

Because of its mid-Atlantic position and good harbour, Horta was a major Allied base during the two world wars. Earlier in history, Faial was attacked and sacked by a British fleet under the Earl of Cumberland in 1589 and again in 1597 by Sir Walter Raleigh and the Earl of Essex. In more peaceful circumstances Captain James Cook called at Faial on a voyage from Newfoundland to England to check his instruments in the garden of "Fredonia", a grand house now used as a children's home.

July and August seem to be the main months to visit Faial, because the island is hopping with festivals, usually religious in nature, but which also celebrate the cultural traditions of the people with food, singing, and dancing. Beautiful island handicrafts, especially lace-work, are also usually on sale.

Then there's Horta's new internationally known Sea Week, celebrated during the first week in August, when yachts from all over the world pour into the harbour to join in races and other sea-based events. The waterfront people join in the celebration, too, by selling specially prepared seafood dishes in little kiosks all round the harbour.

We missed Sea Week, but did what every visiting boat does in this colourful little seaport: headed for Café Sport to meet the granddaddy of all yacht welcomers, Peter Azevedo, subject of comment in books around the world and the man who's made this small mid-Atlantic café better known to cruising yachtsmen than perhaps any other hostelry in the world. He soon demonstrated the warmth that has made him famous.

"Your name's Peter, too?" he asked our youngest. "Well, you certainly deserve a candy."

Azevedo started his career fifty years ago when the arrival of every boat in Faial was a major event. As a teenager, Peter would row out to greet the visiting yachts and personally deliver the mail. What a public-relations gesture!

"Their first question was always, 'Where is Café Sport?'" he told us. "And I was so proud to say it belonged to my father."

Young Peter would take the yachtsmen ashore, where his father would help clear every yacht through customs. And though they no longer do this, their helpful attitude prevails, and clearing customs at Horta today is an easy and relaxed procedure.

We were interested to learn that this international welcomer of trans-Atlantic sailors has never been on a yacht himself!

"Just meeting the yachtsmen has been enough for me," says Azevedo. "Café Sport is my entire life."

And even if the welcome nowadays is not quite as personal as it was when Peter's father founded the first Café Sport in 1918, you'll soon find yourself drinking an espresso or one of Peter's justly famed 35-cent gin and tonics within a few hours of mooring, and talking to other sailors from around the globe.

It was here we met Camille Alibert from France, who had lost his wife and daughter in a bad storm near the Azores five years previously. He and his daughter's husband had managed to make it onto their life raft and had been picked up by a freighter a few days later, but the two women had lost their lives. Alibert continued to sail and now was back in Horta, driven there three months previously by a storm in which he was dismasted.

In the same bar, with its distinctive carved wooden eagle, we heard the story of the desolate steel boat we had seen standing like a lonely sentinel on the beach. The boat had drifted near Horta with a dead man tied to the mast, and painted signs along the decks saying, "No food. No water."

But we preferred not to think of these freak accidents of the sea; after all, the other twenty yachts currently in harbour in sunny September had arrived as safely as we had.

From Slocum onwards, all the cruising greats have passed through this harbour, which added to the excitement we had on landing here, a feeling that "we're one of them". Eric and Susan Hiscock first came here in 1955, returning in 1967; Sir Francis

Chichester, aboard *Gypsy Moth*, visited in 1960 and 1971, and Eric Taberley on *Pen Duick II* dropped anchor here in 1966.

In the thirties, only four or five yachts visited these islands. Then came the war, with yachts only reappearing in the late forties. By the early sixties, things began to get busier, with about ten yachts arriving annually. Then came the yachting explosion the rest of the world was also beginning to experience, and by the mid-seventies – partly caused by the arrival on the world scene of easily attainable self-steering gear – more than 200 yachts were visiting Horta.

The trend continues. In 1983 we were the 545th yacht to add our hand-painted boat portrait to Faial's famous seawall. As well as the boat pictures, the quay is also known for its frequent gatherings of bulls and steers, awaiting shipment to the mainland, and Paul wrote himself into island history by standing firm in the path of a runaway bull. No, he's not a matador, but he is the son of a farmer, and when the bull got loose and started charging down the quay, scattering fishermen and yachtsmen alike, Paul jumped from *Lorcha* and stood in its path, knees bent, arms outstretched. It's the way they stopped bulls on the farm.

"He won't go on charging," explained Paul. "He'll stop and try to get round you – and then you move to the side with him." He was right. The dance continued, to the sound of cheering yachties, until two rather astonished herdsmen ran up to collect their runaway.

But if there were charging bulls to stop, there were also sights to see in the Azores. We took the crowded local ferry across the narrow strip of water between Horta and the island of Pico. After a quick 10-cent espresso in the waterfront café in Magdalena, we were off on the local bus. Winding roads took us through colourful villages and past hundreds of small vineyards protected from the sea winds by walls of volcanic stone. On the country roads, the main transportation was by mule or donkey. If the animal was not carrying any goods, the man usually sat side-saddle, while his wife walked behind. We even saw women carrying baskets on their heads.

Soon we were in Lajes and the small shed-like studio of José

Dimas. Paul was interested in meeting him because of the exquisite two-feet-long whaling boats he carves out of tola wood. We had seen them on display in the tourist office and hotels, but there did not seem to be any available in the local stores. As we watched Dimas in his crowded little workshop sanding and shaping a hull, and carefully nailing a covering board to the topsides, we soon found out why.

This master craftsman, whose work is displayed in museums as far away as Massachussetts and Montevideo, is able to make only six boats every three months, working twelve hours a day. The exquisite vessels come complete with hand-sewn sails, oars, and whaling harpoons. They cost $150 each and there is a long waiting-list for them.

Dimas used to be a stone-carver and didn't start working with wood until he was thirty years old. He became a craftsman after a childhood bout with meningitis made it difficult for him to concentrate on reading and writing. Instead, he was given things to make with his hands. He still does not read, and does not write much more than his name. Now in his fifties, he is about to face another test: he is going blind.

We crossed the island, climbing up and around Pico's landmark mountain – amazingly, the highest in all of Portugal – and down the other side to San Roque, famous as the last and now the only whaling station still operating in the Azores. It was a far cry from the nineteenth-century heyday of whaling, when the islands provided a base for Yankee whalers sailing out of ports like New Bedford and Salem. We had heard that even the remaining whaling boats in Pico and Horta rarely go out, as the station has a glut of whale oil, but the hoot of a steam engine in the distance and a strong smell in the air told us something was happening.

"This is going to look very bloody and not very nice," I warned Peter and Penny. "I think we may see a whale being butchered. If you don't want to see it, we'll leave you here and come back in ten minutes."

"I think we should go," said Penny.

68

"Why do they kill whales here?" asked Peter. "They don't kill whales in Canada."

There were, in fact, two dead sperm whales. They seemed to have been cut into major pieces already – the severed heads lay together at the top of the concrete runway, up which their bodies were dragged. The bodies were in huge sectioned pieces, and dozens of men were attacking each section, hacking off the white blubber, which was loaded into carts and taken inside the factory. The blood streamed down the concrete and into the sea, attracting both fish and fishermen, the rich red colour stretching out at least thirty feet from shore and meeting the blue of the ocean in a startlingly "beautiful" contrast.

Two old steam engines were pressed into service from time to time, their mournful shrieks heralding the hauling of another gigantic lump of flesh further up the runway and nearer the bottomless carts. The intestines had been pulled out and put to one side. The whole place stank, and we were not sorry to leave.

There were quite different sights to see in our last Azorian port of call, São Miguel. The island seemed bigger and richer than the others we visited, and certainly there was a far larger market of fresh produce. Beef and pork were available every day instead of only two days a week, and we found double cream in the stores, a rarity that all of the yachtsmen were rushing to buy.

We were interested in the island's history of making wooden toys and asked the local tourist office to direct us to some toy-makers. There was a polite hesitation. Most of today's toys are made in the local prison! So off we all went – Penny and Peter included. We waited in the large prison lobby and the prisoner craftsmen were brought out to us, one at a time. The finer toys, we found, sell for about a quarter of the price charged in the tourist shops in Ponta Delgada.

This is a lively little port, with narrow streets, bustling stores, and mooring alongside a pontoon. Lace, embroidery, and pottery – not to mention wooden toys and double cream – seem to be the main tourist items.

We were disappointed not to make it to the island of Santa

Maria, just south of São Miguel, where Columbus and his crew came ashore to hear mass on their way back from discovering America in 1492. But we left the Azores happily surprised by all the interesting things we had seen and the fine time we had had. If the other islands we planned on visiting were half as enjoyable, then *Lorcha*'s sail around the Atlantic was going to be a very fine one indeed.

But now, topped up with fresh supplies, we were making straight for Madeira, about five hundred miles southeast.

MAKING MERRY
IN MADEIRA

9

An English adventurer, or an honest-to-goodness, recorded-in-the-history-books Portuguese explorer? Who really first set foot on Madeira?

Some claim that the islands were known to the Romans, who called them the Purple Islands. Sober history records the island's discovery by the Portuguese sailor and explorer João Gonçalves Zarco, who formally claimed "A ilha da Madeira" (an island of wood) on behalf of Prince Henry the Navigator of Portugal in 1420.

We liked the story of Robert Machim much better. He was out for a sail from England when he was shipwrecked on Madeira – along with his mistress, one Ana de Arfet – in 1346. They both liked the wooded island so much (the legend ignores the fact they must have been lacking a boat at this point) that they elected to stay, founding the village of Machico.

They were not the only famous seamen to land on this lush island. According to records of the time, Christopher Columbus made three voyages to Madeira, the first in 1478 or '79 as a sugar merchant, for then (as now) Madeira did a brisk trade in sugar-cane with Europe. Columbus clearly enjoyed his visits, for he later returned to marry Filipa Moniz, daughter of a local governor. They lived in Funchal for a time while Columbus studied various theories of discoveries – obviously successfully, as this was just a few years before his 1492 discovery of America. He later

Zarco, Machim, Columbus . . . Funchal harbour . . . the black
espada . . . unusual mountain ride . . . twenty-year-old brandy . . .
wok cooking . . . family boats . . . valleys and villages . . .
drying shark

---

returned in 1498, and the street where he stayed with João Esmeraldo, a prosperous Flemish sugar merchant, still bears the name of the great adventurer.

After a successful sail from the Azores, we were feeling quite adventurous ourselves as we approached the brightly lit harbour of Funchal under sail at about four o'clock in the morning. Anchoring in the rough waters of the outer harbour was not for us, however, so we made our way cautiously into the small, protected – and very full – fishermen's harbour to starboard as we entered the main port.

There was no berth for another yacht in the already crowded space, and so we tied against a fishing boat and turned in. At 5 a.m. we were wakened because the fishing boat had to move. We lay against another one. The same thing happened at 7 a.m. All morning we manoeuvred about in the small space, looking, so to speak, for a good parking-spot, and at 2 p.m. our patience paid off. We saw a yacht making ready to pull out, and swiftly motored into the vacant spot. We were snug and safe – and we all promptly went to bed to catch up on our sleep, wishing that the new marina we could see under construction were completed for our benefit.

After clearing in with Customs and Immigration on the waterfront, we did what most yachtsmen do on arriving in a new town, especially those with children – we looked for a bakery and the market! Madeiran bread is varied and wonderful, and a special treat at the bakeries is the big jars of very reasonably priced home-made cookies.

73

Funchal was the first European city to be built in the Atlantic islands, and it takes its name from the fennel that grows everywhere. Perhaps appropriately, its fruit-and-vegetable market is a nine-day wonder, a huge area jam-packed with a wide variety of fruit and vegetables as well as fresh eggs and a huge selection of flowers. The small stores around the market carry all the other groceries anyone is likely to need.

At the south end of the market we stood on the wide stairs leading down to the remarkable fish market and looked over the catch of the day. The special feature is the black espada, a fearsome-looking large-toothed fish, which looks like a long, fat black eel, and lives at a depth of 600 metres (2,000 feet). It's astonishing to think of the fishermen hooking the fish at those enormous depths – by hand-lining! The fish is light, white, and delicious eating.

The island is also well known for its wicker industry. It seems that in Madeira you can get almost any article of furniture or decoration made from the supple willow branches that grow in profusion along the roadside. We would have loved some of this stuff for our house in Canada – but it was not, unfortunately, suitable for a 30-foot boat!

The wicker is made into about five hundred different kinds of baskets. In the sixteenth century somebody had the bright idea of building baskets big enough to carry people, in the style of a toboggan. And in particular, big enough to carry intrepid passengers down the steep slopes of the mountains behind Funchal!

Today the ride, covering a 2,000-foot vertical drop, is a considerable tourist attraction. We took a bus up the hills to Monté, and while the other tourists went into the large café in the main square, we wandered into the steep side streets and found the tiny second-floor bar where the sled-runners gather to eat each day. Dressed in white shirts, hats, and pants, with special boots to protect their feet, the men politely bunched up together at one table to make room for us. Soon we were eating the thick, rich meat soup that was obviously the dish of the day. In deference to our special status as visitors, our bread was

74

neatly sliced for us. The runners were served whole large crusty loaves, one to a man.

Fortified by lunch, Paul, Penny, and Peter got into one sled – while I followed behind. Two men were assigned to each basket, which they controlled with ropes at the side and also with their feet, jumping on and off the runners. Sometimes they had to give us a bit of a push – but mostly the baskets flew down the narrow, winding cobblestone roads, and occasionally the men rode the steep passages perched on the runners. It was definitely faster than walking.

We got off about halfway down because we wanted to walk through the suburbs of Funchal. The steep downhill streets were just wide enough for two small cars, and were lined with small terraced houses, each one laden with a profusion of flowers, which tempted us to linger and admire.

Paul was striding along ahead when he was hailed from a narrow doorway. We stopped and looked in. The interior was inviting – and it was full of wine barrels.

"Come in. Come in," said a voice in excellent English. "We have just discovered a twenty-year-old barrel of brandy. Would you like to try some?"

Madeirans, we had already discovered, are friendly people, and visitors are made very welcome. In the harbour the sport fishing boats' crews had cut us thick steaks of wahoo, in the breadstore the baker invariably handed Penny and Peter a cookie sample, and at one restaurant a couple sitting near us had given the children a large golden honey-cake, a Madeiran specialty.

Now we were having an afternoon of brandy-tasting – and enjoying the company of Fernando and Isabel Rodriguez. Fernando's father, who had died two years earlier, had been a fine wine-maker. On Madeira this means a great deal. The islands were originally famed for wood and then sugar-cane, but above all for wine. Madeira wine is reputed to have been very popular in England by the sixteenth century and a favourite of Queen Elizabeth I herself. It is said that Napoleon's exile was somewhat eased by the British Consul's gift of cases of Madeira when the former Emperor's escort stopped in Funchal on the way to Saint Helena.

Feeling very mellow, we toured the house. What had looked like a small dwelling from the outside turned out to be a large farm, especially large by Madeiran standards, where land is so scarce that every available plot is neatly terraced. Because the house had been in the family for many years, we were also able to wonder at the valuable old wooden wine-making equipment and other antique pieces strewn casually around the spacious cellars.

Outside we toured the banana trees and the christolphe (a green vegetable that grows on a vine) plantation, and met the two cows living in their personal shed, as all cattle in Madeira do, since on the steep cultivated terraces it is too dangerous to let cattle wander. We were all having such a good time that, happily accepting a huge basket of fresh vegetables for the boat, I invited the Rodriguezes to dinner aboard *Lorcha*.

"Certainly not," roared Fernando. "You must have dinner with us first. You are in our country."

Sometimes it's hard to repay hospitality when you're travelling, but the Rodriguezes, their friend Esther, and their nine-year-old son, Michael, did visit us later in the week, and I used *Lorcha's* special cooking weapon to provide an unusual dinner.

We carry a wok and various Chinese ingredients on board in order to surprise guests with an Oriental meal. I started out with three special dishes – lemon garlic chicken, pork saté (which is really Indonesian), and chicken in soy sauce with peanuts, but of course we soon discovered that fish dishes also cook up really well in the wok. From being a specialty utensil, the wok has developed into something we now use for about half our cooking. It heats fast and cooks quickly, and we know that stir-fry fresh vegetables retain more vitamins than boiled vegetables.

Finding Chinese ingredients around the Atlantic islands has not been as difficult as I had feared. We were to find Chinese communities and stores in the Canaries, Brazil, French Guiana,

Trinidad and Tobago, and Venezuela. So I have never run out of soy sauce and have always been able to stock up with such necessary fresh ingredients as fresh garlic, ginger, sesame oil, Chinese cooking wine, and black-bean paste.

The special Chinese noodles and the chopsticks we carried helped round out the meal in Madeira. The Rodriguez family were especially delighted, because, despite the fact that Funchal has many international restaurants and no fewer than six five-star hotels, there are few Chinese restaurants, so the unusual meal was a treat.

Funchal is the first gathering-point for European sailors on the trade-wind route to the Caribbean. So there were always at least fifty cruising vessels in the harbour, and boats came and went every day flying Norwegian, Swedish, South African, Danish, Dutch, and Belgian flags, with the most common being German, French, and British. We were always having interesting conversations with boats from other lands as we shuttled between our boat and the shore in our trusty dinghy. This was the first harbour in which we saw other boats with children, so the to-ing and fro-ing between the family vessels was constant. Taking half a dozen children ashore for an excursion to the natural rock swimming-pool at one end of town or to the newly built Lido complex at the other was a weekly event, with other boat parents reciprocating, and there was a great deal of boat-to-boat visiting.

This was also the first harbour in which we met a really unhappy family boat. British-registered, with a couple and four pre-teen children aboard, the boat was headed for the Caribbean. He had taken early retirement and put the family's life savings into the voyage. Now she was threatening to pull out, with the children being yanked between. The problem was quite deep. He was determined to get to the Caribbean, but couldn't manage the 47-foot boat by himself, especially if some of the children elected to stay with him; but she was also trapped, as she had no money of her own and no access to the family bank account.

We spent a lot of time with the kids and had them all over to

77

supper one night while the parents went out to dinner to try to settle their differences. They came back at midnight, full of wine and goodwill, and we toasted their future happy voyage to the Caribbean two days later.

We never saw them again, though their fragile pact evidently soon shattered under the strain of the rough voyaging at this time of year. Boats in Tenerife passed on stories of the fights and rows on board not long after they arrived in the Canaries. It was a warning of the perils of family cruising when things go sour.

But, this one boat apart, our stay in Madeira was a very pleasant one. The harbour was near the centre of town, which made for easy daily shopping and interesting walks along the waterfront.

The island's interior is great for exploring, as it is filled with volcanic craters which form superb, albeit steep, mountains and valleys. Cheap and reliable buses drive to great heights with dramatic views of precipitous drops to a valley floor or ocean bed. The drops are so steep that the experience is not recommended for anyone who suffers in the slightest degree from vertigo, and they left us gasping.

One interior village we visited was Curral das Freias, a collection of houses in a valley two thousand feet above the sea. As in all these interior towns, you can walk almost anywhere in the surrounding hills, following the well-worn paths still used by the locals. As we puffed our way up and down one steep path, people carrying goods from one village to the next (6 kilometres away in this case) passed us on the run. Solid leg muscles were in evidence on people aged from seven to seventy! And healthy though we consider ourselves to be with our bracing outdoor life, we could not compete in this mountain race, and stood back smiling admiringly at everyone who passed us.

Two picturesque places within easy bus distance of Funchal are the coastal villages of Ribeiro Brava, with its waterfront market of embroideries and hand-made sweaters and open-air espada market on the seafront, and Camara de Lobos, the centre of the espada fishing industry, and the home of hundreds of seals (lobos) when Zarco first sailed into its rocky natural harbour.

"Look at all that laundry over there," said Penny, pointing across the bay. "Doesn't it look funny?"

It looked so strange that a walk around the bay was in order, and a closer look showed us we had found, not laundry, but a thriving small shark-drying industry.

But it was nearing time to be under sail again, as we wanted to make some interior changes to the boat in the Canary Islands, our next stop. It was a real shame; even though Paul had put hours of work into lovingly constructing a head (boat terminology for toilet) in which he could stand, he was going to tear the whole thing apart in Las Palmas on Gran Canaria, 280 miles south of Madeira, though our first stop would be Tenerife.

"Do we need a comfortable toilet – or enough space to store cookies for every day when we cross to Brazil?" I asked the crew democratically.

"Cookies," shouted Peter and Penny.

FRIENDS IN
THE CANARIES

10

At dawn *Lorcha* sailed quietly into Tenerife in the Canary Islands, our senses telling us what it must have been like in that same harbour when the eleven ships from England, now known as the First Fleet, made Tenerife their first port of call in 1787. The fleet was bound for Australia with the first shipment of 750 convicts who were to settle in Botany Bay. At the helm was Captain Arthur Phillip, who was to be the governor of the new British penal colony in New South Wales. Squaresails flying and topsails set, they must have made an impressive entrance into this quiet harbour.

It is not known what welcome they were accorded, but ten years later, in 1797, Admiral Horatio Nelson suffered the only defeat of his career when his English fleet was repulsed, leaving their captured banners to be displayed in the Carta Chapel. We didn't expect cannonfire, but our guidebooks on the Tenerife harbour of Santa Cruz said visiting yachts were not particularly welcome at the local yacht club and should make for the fishing-boat harbour. We imagined a small rocky inlet with a few boats.

What a surprise.

The Canary Islands have a population of over a million – far more than the Azores or Madeira – and this is a huge international fishing port. Tuna trawlers from lands as far away as the Soviet Union and Korea lined the docks. In the far distance there were scores of

80

---

yachts, so many that we all made headline news in the local Tenerife paper that morning: "More than 80 yachts are currently moored in Santa Cruz harbour waiting to cross the Atlantic – the most boats there have ever been there."

What is especially nice about sailing to new harbours these days is that we recognize boats and people we have met in other harbours. English single-hander V.J. waved to us from his 16-foot *Felix*; Oliver and Claire from Brittany, France, whose boat we were aboard in Funchal, greeted us merrily; and Lilly and Reg from Belgium followed us in. We moored between a German boat which had sailed from Australia and a returning U.S. vessel with a doctor, a psychiatrist, and a lawyer aboard (no jokes, please).

We also spied our first Canadian flag, and lost no time in meeting Andy and Carolyn Van Herk aboard their custom-built 40-foot Frank Madrick wooden ketch *Eryngo*. The Van Herks had been sailing for nine years, had covered sixty thousand miles, and now had only to cross the Atlantic Ocean to complete a circumnavigation. Penny and Peter's eyes popped when six-year-old Sandi and four-year-old Chad appeared out of the cabin to see what the noise was about. A few minutes later, out tumbled eighteen-month-old Tami. These three blond-haired children – two born in the Virgin Islands and one in Australia – have never known a life other than living on a sailboat. The five children were soon engrossed in one another's company.

At dusk, sitting in *Eryngo's* comfortable cockpit, it was easy to tell that the Van Herks had travelled far. We nibbled poppadums from Sri Lanka, and dipped them in sesame-seed paste from Egypt, then tasted the olives they had picked and pickled in Greece, and topped things off with rum from Gibraltar and tonic water from Spain.

We got on so well with the Van Herks that the two families decided to rent a car together for two days to see the sights. Budget-conscious as ever, we rented a small five-seat car to hold all nine of us. (Living on a boat does accustom one to making do with a small space!) One of the high points of our drive around the island was a visit to the perpetually snow-capped peak of the Tiede, the highest mountain in Spain. We spent several hours climbing over the rough lava fields where the NASA moon buggy underwent testing before carrying the astronauts to the Tiede-like surface of the moon.

Tenerife harbour was a pleasant stopping-off place, with a large area for children to play in, frequent bus service to town, and a short walk to a pleasant beach and a small village with a do-it-yourself outdoor scrub-board laundry – not perfect, but better than *Lorcha*'s facilities.

There are many harbours to visit in the seven-island group of the Canaries, but we only moored in Tenerife and, with some trepidation, in Las Palmas on Gran Canaria. This latter was described by cruising sailor and writer Donald Street in his *Cruising Guide to the Eastern Caribbean, Vol. I* (1980 edition) as "one of the dirtiest harbours in the world".

He adds:

"Get into it, do your business and get out in a hurry. It is a harbour to be avoided."

Fighting words, but no longer true – fortunately for the trans-Atlantic sailor who wants to visit what must be one of the best stocking-up ports in the world. This is not to say Las Palmas would get an award for cleanliness, but both the harbour and the four-year-old marina, under its manager, Nicasio Suarez Garcia, have made great strides in providing much-improved facilities for the long-distance cruiser, and in putting out a welcome mat. Now, on pulling into Las Palmas, you can expect to find mooring-places, showers, garbage containers, and a marina waterfront bar. Expansion plans for new moorings were in the works when we visited, for the number of yachts coming into Las Palmas has doubled every year since 1980.

Stocking up on drinking-water is still a problem in Las Palmas, since the water is mostly desalinated and, though drinkable, tastes from tolerable to terrible. Occasionally fresh rainwater comes through the hose – and when that happens, it's time to spread the word and fill every jerry can in sight.

Las Palmas is also a central crew pick-up and exchange spot. Almost every day we would see a hopeful new traveller with a backpack doing the rounds of the boats and asking if anyone wanted crew. Some sought passage to the Caribbean. Some wanted a lift to Brazil. Some just wanted to join a boat for a year.

The port was also the scene of many crew changes as people hopped from one boat to another. In fact, keeping track of changing crew was rather like watching a soap opera, as unhappy captains evicted crew they didn't want any more, knowing there were many applicants available, and disgruntled crew members flounced off other boats declaring the captain a pig and the food abominable – and usually finding passage on board another boat within a week or two.

Two friends of ours were eagerly awaiting the crew they had advertised for in a British yachting magazine. They were a couple who wanted a third person with them on their first Atlantic crossing. Out of eighty applicants, they had carefully chosen a woman with no sailing experience ("she'll be more likely to do what she's told"), who was a mountain climber ("she'll be fit") and who displayed a certain sense of humour in her application.

Unfortunately the young woman who arrived was rather overweight, full of her own importance, and strangely reluctant to follow orders. She also wore extremely low-cut T-shirts. The captain's wife was not happy.

The climax came one day when the captain ordered her to tie off the bosun's chair halyard so that he wouldn't slide thirty feet to the deck. Outraged, she left him dangling on his chair halfway up the mast, while she debated carrying out his instructions in a voice that carried all over the harbour.

"I don't know why you think you can give me orders," she bellowed as the captain's wife rushed to secure the dangling chair halyard. "I will not be treated like a child."

She showed absolutely no sense of humour when the captain withdrew his offer of passage across the Atlantic. This rather unlikely crew member was last seen walking up the gangplank of an Australian boat with two adults who were only too glad to take a third person with them to help out with ocean watches. Somewhere in Australia, there's a couple with an interesting story to tell. . . .

Las Palmas is a big Spanish city with everything a big city has to offer, and with the added advantage that it is a duty-free port. It is rather astonishing to see the large selection of goods here when one has spent months visiting only small islands.

There are a number of very good fruit-and-vegetable markets which also sell fresh fish and meat. Certainly, if he had been given the option, Columbus would have stocked up at one of the Las Palmas supermarkets, and not on the tiny island of Gomera, before setting out to discover America.

We did not make many excursions around Las Palmas because we were busy with our alterations to the boat. But one attraction Penny and Peter enjoyed was the beautiful little Christopher Columbus Museum at the southern end of the city. Columbus visited the islands three times in the 1490s, and there is pride in the connection. By now, the children knew a lot about this early navigator, and it was exciting for them to see his navigation instruments, replicas of his ships, and the old maps tracing his voyages.

We were walking idly along the dock on our first day in Las Palmas, looking over the approximately fifty boats tied stern-to, when Paul spotted a 40-foot yawl called *Magic Dragon*.

"I think we were moored alongside that boat in Turkelimanos," he said. I was astonished. We were moored in that small fishing harbour in Greece in 1976!

Just then a silver-haired man came up the companionway still talking to his wife below. Paul remembers boats. I remember voices, and immediately recognized Joe Silverman's strong Boston accent. A few minutes later we were all sitting aboard *Magic Dragon* talking as if the intervening years had never happened. We had spent less than a week in the same harbour with the Silvermans, visiting each other's boats and sharing a waterfront meal of octopus and squid. Now, seven years later, we were greeting each other like old friends, proof of the fact that you form intense friendships when you are cruising.

"You had quite an effect on our lives," said Joe, smiling. "We sailed north to Turkey because you had said it was so nice up there, and after reading your articles I decided to do some writing – and I've had a series of articles published."

"I'm glad you recognized us," said Miriam. "We might not have connected the carefree young couple we met in Greece with the responsible parents with two children we saw walking past the boat."

Meeting people and forming friendships afloat is different from making friendships ashore. For a start, it's almost ridiculously easy to meet other yachties. Where are you from? Can I take a line? Do you know where to get fresh bread? How long have you been here? All are simple and natural openers. One thing leads to another, and before long you've decided whether you want to spend more time with the people you are talking with – or to get on with your projects for the day.

Everyone is in transit, so if friendships are to be made, there is no time to be lost. Boats come and go in harbour every day. Tonight may be the only time you can spend a couple of hours with someone. So a coffee, drink, or dinner invitation will often be made within ten minutes of meeting someone.

Everyone is travelling on a budget – and even though some budgets are fatter than others, people are always willing to share. Great to have dinner with you – can I bring dessert?

Our shop-talk is, of course, sailing. And unlike conversations in the big city, where one partner is often working at the office, with the other at home, sailing is of interest to everyone. New harbours, adventures on the way, how the children are coping, the next stop – it's talk to which everyone can contribute.

Long-distance cruisers are a hard-working lot. Contrary to the stereotype of yachtsmen lying around the boat all day with a drink in one hand, during daylight hours we're usually working quite hard on our boats. Ocean crossings take their toll. Torn sails have to be sewn, lashings have to be checked, supplies must be bought and stowed away.

Our main projects in Las Palmas were changing Paul's beloved toilet with its standing headroom into a storage area with 10-litre containers for flour, sugar, rice, and cornmeal, and creating a new toilet in a very small space forward by the mast. Poor Paul! Maybe our next boat will be bigger . . .

We were lucky to find sturdy, 10-litre, large-opening, screw-top plastic containers in Las Palmas and we fitted six of them into our new storage area. That done, and the new toilet installed, we sewed a rain-catcher – not strictly necessary for catching rain at sea (maximum passages in the Atlantic are under thirty days), but good for replenishing one's water supply in harbour. And on the ocean, one never knows.

Las Palmas was a wonderful stopping-off place for Penny and Peter, since this was a port where the boat was tied to a dock, making it easy for the kids to get ashore, and where there were also a number of family boats. In such a situation we're happy to let the kids wander, though we have some rules for their behaviour ashore.

But kids are kids, and it was in Las Palmas that we went through the rather frightening experience of having Peter go missing.

TRAVELLING KIDS

11

"I wish you'd write something about safety for children aboard boats," said Frank Szerdanely, father of seven-year-old Paul and nine-year-old Cathy, and captain of the 32-foot sloop *Interlude* from San Francisco. The subject was very much on my mind as Peter and his friend Paul Szerdanely had been the subject of a dock search that very afternoon.

We had done all the usual things beforehand. When we come into a new harbour, we like to walk around the marina with the children to check things out, give them limits to wander in, and also to get the feel of our new mooring-place. Lots of children – great. Large concrete area for them to play in – great. Lighthouse for them to walk to – good. Very large rocks running about five hundred yards on the other side of the pier, with caves and underground tunnels. Hmmm. Looks fun, but might be dangerous.

In Las Palmas we introduced ourselves and Penny and Peter to a few boats that had children aboard. That way, all the family boats would be able to identify them as boat children. And we, in turn, could recognize and place the other boat kids. Then we went through the shore rules.

"Don't leave the boat without letting us know. Watch out for cars on the dock. Don't go aboard any of the other boats without telling us where you are. Do not leave the marina with anyone but us."

Even though the marina was big, from the boat I could more or less see where the groups of children were if I went into the cockpit. I got into the habit of looking out from there about every half-hour, and every so often the kids themselves would run back to *Lorcha*.

It was on just such a casual check five days after we had moored in the marina that I noticed Peter wasn't with the other children.

"Where's Peter?" I asked Penny.

"I don't know," said Penny. "Oh, I think he went off with Paul S."

I walked around the marina once, but couldn't see either of the boys. As they seemed to be together, I wasn't particularly worried, but I went over to the *Interlude* to ask Paul's mother, Nancy, if the boys were on her boat. No luck. Nancy herself then also came out.

I checked the lighthouse area and Nancy climbed over the rocks, while her husband went to the marina centre and the small café, and checked with the other boats. Thirty minutes later, there was still no sign of the boys, so we gathered all the other kids together and asked them to help us look for the boys and show us their favourite playing places. This in itself was a surprise: the children's first-choice playing area was their "secret" tunnel in the rocks, a tunnel covered by water at high tide.

After another fruitless thirty-minute search I was beginning to feel concerned. Nancy, who has been sailing with her children for five years, was worried about a possible water accident. With big-city fears still in the back of my mind, I was more apprehensive about an abduction by car.

At that moment I spotted a speeding dinghy in the harbour,

noticeable because it was moving so fast. As it came closer, I could see young children – and, yes, Peter and Paul S. were aboard.

It was a great relief to find the boys – but I was certainly annoyed with the dinghy-owner, who turned out to be one of the friendly French yachtsmen. It was kind of him to take the children out – but he should have checked with the parents first. And two of the boys, including Peter, were non-swimmers – yet no one had a life-jacket on.

Later I tried to explain to Peter that he must tell me where he is going. Penny was a great help.

"Or tell me," she said in her most caring, sisterly fashion. "I might have wanted to go too."

"You just can't be too careful," said Frank, as we all sat on *Interlude* later that evening, enjoying a shared dinner. "I learned a real lesson when we were in Cyprus. Young Paul handles the dinghy very well by himself and it's fun for him to row it in harbour, though he's got to wear a life-jacket. One day he asked if he could take out two new friends. I said no to the four-year-old, but okay, the six-year-old could go if he put on his life-jacket and checked with his parents. The next thing I saw was someone diving from shore to rescue the kid. It turned out Paul's new friend had started jumping around and the boat had tipped over. He couldn't swim – and he hadn't put on his life-jacket."

Frank had gone over to the boy's parents to tell them what had happened and to apologize for not personally checking that the boy had put on his life-jacket.

"They didn't seem very concerned," he said. "The shocker came two weeks later. Their younger son drowned."

That was the second boat child drowned that year known to the Szerdanelys. We ourselves had seen an eighteen-month-old almost drown in Funchal. The parents were asleep in the sun on deck – while their daughter floated face down in the water, having crawled over the side of the dinghy where she had been left "safely" playing. Shouting fishermen woke the parents just in time.

After all these stories, we sat below decks on *Lorcha* and had a family council, the upshot of which was that Peter agreed to wear his life-jacket when playing ashore, with the promise that the life-jacket would go as soon as he could swim fifty yards by himself. Penny agreed to help monitor Peter and remind him about his jacket if necessary, while Paul and I reinforced his good behaviour for the first week by giving him a small reward every time he remembered to put on his jacket by himself.

It wasn't hard to make the new rule stick and, of course, Peter now had a real incentive to learn to swim, which he did at the first fresh-water swimming-pool we moored near.

Ocean safety was another matter. There was now no question about the wearing of life-jackets. They had to be worn at all times. At sea the children were forbidden to go forward on the bow. In bad weather or after dusk, they had to wear their safety harnesses.

The children learned to obey these instructions without question. Sometimes when Peter crawled out of the cabin in heavy weather without his life-jacket on, it was really hard for him to go below decks by himself to get it, with the boat pitching and tossing. But he had to do it, because usually one parent was on the helm and the other sleeping.

As far as seasickness is concerned, Peter is the lucky one. After his initial bout with seasickness in the North Atlantic, he has not suffered since. On each new ocean passage (until we reached the calmer waters of Brazil), however, Penny was sick for about the first three days. I now give her seasickness tablets at the start of each new voyage. During this time, she no longer stays below decks at all, but sits and takes naps in the cockpit. She'd sleep there too if I'd let her – and I often do on the first night. She eats and drinks very little, and I let her find her own level, though I have to wash out her mouth with water every two or three hours. As soon as she's found her sea legs, she's just fine and eats as much as ever. She then has terrific bursts of energy and goes right back to raising havoc below decks with Peter. She doesn't usually get sick again.

During his three days without a companion, Peter becomes very self-sufficient. He does extraordinarily well at finding things to do below decks. He'll take out his own project books and work away at joining dots, solving mazes, or making up some game with his animals. And he talks to himself constantly. If there was no sound of Peter chattering away, I'd wonder what was wrong.

Our first ocean crossing was a period of intense education for all of us. The most surprising thing for me was the continuous and persistent ocean swell, and the fact that on all our early passages I did no teaching. By the time I had done my watches, cooked, recovered from mal de mer, and generally helped look after the boat and the children, there was simply no time to sit down and do schoolwork with Penny.

There were, however, lots of other things to see and learn. Penny became an avid star-watcher, sitting up with me late at night to watch and identify the constellations and how they moved across the sky. A favourite book was *Stars and Planets*, and it was not long before she knew the names and characteristics of all nine planets, and could recognize the major star constellations.

We did no formal school lessons, but we found it fun to set out on each passage with a special book to read to the children. Robert Louis Stevenson's *Treasure Island* turned out to be a wonderful choice for our first ocean crossing. Eventually we would be sailing to the area where the story took place, and the romance of islands, adventure, and pirate treasure thoroughly entranced the children, who would sit on the floor of the cockpit begging us to read another chapter as soon as one had been finished.

Our next ocean book was also a good choice. Paul had picked up Arthur Ransome's *Swallows and Amazons* at a jumble sale in Toronto just before we left. He did not remember the precise content of the book, but recalled that it had something vaguely to do with boats and water. The children were elated when it turned out to be the story of four teenagers and their adventures on their own sailboat. And the good thing about the book was that it was part of a series, so at our next port the children wrote to their grandmother in Scotland asking for some of the other books for Christmas.

Of course, there were the hard lessons, too. One day Peter lost his favourite yellow drinking-mug overboard. It sank, and he was very upset when he couldn't retrieve it. He went below decks, to reappear about three hours later carrying a piece of cardboard with a string through it.

"This is the life raft for Puppydog, Zebra, Lambie Pie and Paddington," he announced solemnly.

One of the advantages of our new lifestyle was that though our schedule was hectic, we could also make the time to concentrate on activity with the children. Peter was just starting to learn the phonetic sounds of letters when we left Toronto, and when we reached the Azores I decided to make his reading lessons a priority. Like the swimming, we would make a concentrated effort to get to a basic stage. It doesn't take long to teach a child to start reading if you have an excellent tool like Sidney Ledson's *Teach Your Child to Read in 60 Days*.

We planned one session every day, and a second evening session probably every other day. Two and a half months – and five thousand miles – later, Peter could read simple words and sentences like "Today I will have lots of milk".

Both children were excellent students, which is what we hear about most boat children. In port, we did our formal lessons first thing in the morning, right after breakfast, starting at 7:30 or 8 a.m. I taught Penny every day, because she was expected to complete her year's material by July to qualify her for the following year's lessons. I taught Peter most mornings, but not every morning. He was still at kindergarten age, so the fact that he could read and count already rated him ahead of the expected Grade 1 starting level.

Peter's reading lessons took about fifteen minutes, while Penny usually worked for a one-to-two-hour stretch, with Peter looking longingly on at her formal schoolbooks and listening to every word. When Penny read a story aloud and then got tested on her recall and comprehension, I usually included Peter in the sessions.

Penny and I sat side by side at the main cabin table, everything spread out around us. Peter sat on the starboard bunk with his own project. If he interrupted too often, he was banished to write or draw or play on the table-like space on top of the engine box. Not perfect, but at least an alternative space. Paul did the breakfast dishes while we got on with lessons, and sometimes he would take Peter off for a walk or a visit to another boat while Penny and I finished our day's work.

We usually worked every day, including Saturdays and Sundays, as we had plenty of non-working days when we were on the ocean or making a special trip somewhere, which happened quite often, as we liked to go exploring in new countries. Most of these trips turned out to be an education for all of us, with many of them ending up as subject matter for Penny's diary.

The diary started not as an outlet for Penny's imagination, but because she hated her printing lessons.

"Mummy, I like doing mathematics. I love reading, but I can't stand doing this printing. It's so *boring*."

I tried everything. I changed the order of the letters she was supposed to copy. I made up new sentences and words to catch her interest. I told stories about each letter. But I could not get away from the truth. Learning to print is – well – boring.

Then one day when we were ashore in Las Palmas buying some paper supplies, Penny pointed to an attractive diary with a pretty picture on the front.

"What's that for?" she asked.

I explained, and Penny promptly said:

"I'd like to write my own diary."

When we had first left Canada, both children had kept a kind of diary. They would tell me what they thought the highlights of each day were – and I'd write it down. It was the sort of idea that sounded good in theory, but we abandoned it after a few weeks.

On this day, however, we had no sooner got back to *Lorcha* with Penny's new book than she sat down at the main cabin table and said, "What shall I write about?"

We decided that we wouldn't lock ourselves into a daily account, but that she would write about special events and her own adventures as they happened. We always put the name of the place where we were anchored at the head of each story, together with the date. Penny not only had to print all the words

94

in her stories, but I told her that she had to think of what she wanted to say by herself.

"I think I can do it, Mummy," she said. "But how do I begin?"

I thought of myself writing my first story for a Toronto theatre magazine at age twenty-five – and asking the editor the exact same question.

"Pretend you've just come back and you want to tell me what you did. Just tell me what you saw – and write it down," I said. "Start with the most exciting thing."

Penny was able to spell the easy words by herself, only asking me for help with the more difficult ones. Her first four-sentence story took about an hour to write, but we were both ecstatic. She loved the idea of writing, and did not even seem to realize she was doing her boring printing. Soon, however, the fact that she was printing became almost incidental, although the printing was the neatest she had ever done. Penny was learning to organize her thoughts, write out place names and dates, and consolidate her spelling. Artwork also came into it. She drew pictures of her experiences, chose photographs for her stories from my contact sheets, suggested postcards when she saw one that would fit her story, and used stamps, cut-outs, and paper money to give variety and texture to her words.

Her ability at self-expression led to another art – letter-writing. Her godmother, grandmothers, and favourite aunts began to receive well-written notes about sailing, animals, and visits to other boats. (Not to be outdone, Peter sent pictures!)

The diaries – Penny's now on her second – are nothing out of the ordinary. Words are misspelt, numbers are occasionally written backwards, and some stories are better than others. They're the thoughts of a six-year-old, now seven. But because they're simple, easy to read, and well illustrated, they're the best summary account of our 12,000-mile voyage.

Penny may never be one of the best printers in her class, but she'll probably be one of the only kids to have a story book date-lined Las Palmas, Cape Verdes, Fernando de Noronha, The Amazon, Tobago, Venezuela, Bonaire, and Panama.

A WILD PASSAGE

12

All our ocean passages in the Atlantic seemed to focus on a different experience – and our 840-mile sail from Las Palmas to Mindelo in the Cape Verdes was no exception. It was a *wild* one.

This has traditionally been a wild coast, of course, and one that struck terror into the hearts of the earliest explorers. When Prince Henry the Navigator of Portugal established his school of navigation and exploration at Sagres, everything about it was kept as secret as a modern space station, and anyone misappropriating charts would be put to death. But one aspect of Henry's aims was not secret. His plan was not to discover lands in the west, but to send Portuguese ships down the coast of Africa so far that they would discover a route to the spice lands of the east.

The area between the Canaries and the Cape Verdes was the great barrier, called by Arab geographers "the Green Sea of Darkness", from which there was no return. To the superstitious sailors of the day that was not inviting. "Why," they are supposed to have asked the exasperated Henry, "should we attempt to pass the limits that our forefathers established?" Year after year, poor Henry sent bold skippers down that coast only to have them return defeated, until in 1432 Gil Eannes passed Cabo Bojador, and lived to tell the tale.

Green Sea of Darkness . . . fair-wind wait . . . ocean routines . . .
halfway mark . . . fish at last . . . drifting freighter . . . big waves . . .
navigation mystery . . . São Antão appears . . . dolphin escort

---

After that, the Portuguese explorers slowly advanced decade by decade until in 1456 Cadamosto discovered the Cape Verdes – and in 1487 Diaz rounded the Cape of Good Hope.

Now we were eager to try our luck with the Green Sea of Darkness. For thirteen long days we had waited for the wind to stop blowing from the southwest – the direction we wanted to go. A northeast wind at last puffed cautiously on the morning of January 3, mounting steadily all day until it reached gale force during the night. The next day the wind was blowing 20 to 25 knots, but at least it was behind us. Undeterred, we waved goodbye to many friends, most of whom would be sailing west to the Caribbean, and set off from Las Palmas.

There was no doubt that the wind had been much stronger the previous night, for a freighter and a barge lay newly driven on the rocks in the outer harbour. As we sailed out we had to steer our way through the now-floating cargo of barrels and other debris. There was still a heavy swell, so Penny and I took our seasickness medication immediately. Better safe than sorry. And as usual we gave the children their "first-day, once-clear-of-the-harbour" surprise package – this time a little cardboard village to colour and then put together. As usual, too, Paul and I knew that we would be slightly groggy for a few days as our bodies adapted to our three-hours-on and three-hours-off night watches.

Later that first day we heard that the wind had gusted to seventy-two knots the previous night on the nearby island of Lanzarote. Clearly, a good night to spend in the harbour! But the wind was still strong enough to keep us sailing with three panels reefed, and the swells continued to give us trouble, with both Paul and Peter getting sick. I put Peter on suppositories (real ones this time). But once Paul has actually brought everything up, he seems to recover quickly.

The wind was now blowing directly behind us and we were in some danger of accidentally gybing – the wind (or a wave) might cause the sail to swing violently across the boat – so we sailed first to one side of our direct course (30 degrees in this case) and then changed direction by swinging the sail over in a controlled manner to point the boat in a complementary direction on the other side of our direct course. This meant that the boat sailed 30 degrees off course with each tack, but with the wind no longer dead aft, the motion was much steadier and the boat more controllable. We would sail a zigzag course to our destination, thus adding miles to our passage, but also adding comfort and safety.

By the fourth morning, Penny and Peter were up and bouncing around the cockpit, but it was not until the fifth day that we were all well enough to start our regular full-time routine at sea – sunsights and position fixes at least twice a day, cooking proper meals, and enjoying general family get-togethers in the cockpit without one or two people sleeping below.

Lorcha had been averaging 120 miles per day in the 20- to-30-knot winds even though the sail had been reefed four and even five out of a total of seven panels. We're always ready to reef early in heavy weather. It doesn't make much difference to the speed of the boat, but it certainly makes for comfort to have less canvas up when the boat starts heeling. When the weather abated on the fifth day, we raised the sail panel by panel until, for the first time on the trip, we were under full sail and still making good speed, despite the lessening wind.

That same day we passed the halfway mark, which we celebrated with an instant blancmange pudding (it tastes so delicious at sea) and with our now traditional halfway surprise for Penny and Peter – slim coloured markers. At 7 p.m. Paul had another surprise for us.

"I've got a fish," he sang out.

The kids threw down their markers and scrambled up the companionway. Could the most inexpert fishing yacht on the high seas have actually hooked something? Of course, we had bought a super new blue squid lure in Tenerife – complete with optimistic 100-pound test line!

Paul took in the trailing log (so it wouldn't tangle) and shouted to me to get *Lorcha* hove-to, not moving forward but with the sail steadying her. He had 100 metres of heavy fishing-line to pull in, and couldn't get what felt like a big one on board with the boat continuing to surge ahead. Chaos reigned. Paul pulled in the line hand over hand, foot by foot – with the kids "helping" inch by inch, both of them anxious to be part of the excitement. Soon twisted monofilament line covered the cockpit. Watching the three musketeers with some amusement, I misjudged the wind and accidentally swung the boat round in a circle. The line and fish disappeared under the hull.

"For God's sake," said Paul in exasperation – it was, after all, his first catch. "Do you guys want this fish or not?"

We were all laughing so much that it was a wonder we ever got out of the mess, but, with a final heave, there she was – a beautiful ten-pound tuna.

"Let's get the fish book and look it up," said Penny, eager and scholarly as ever, as I dived below for the camera. We had never caught a fish before – and who knows when we might hook another one? I wanted to record the catch!

"It's a bluefin, I think," said Penny, leafing through the book. "Did you know that the largest rod-caught bluefin was hooked near Prince Edward Island and it weighed 1,120 pounds? How much does ours weigh?"

We laughed. Though our fish was some eleven hundred pounds short of the mark, a ten-pound catch is still a lot of fish for a small boat and would last us a couple of days. The children watched phlegmatically as Paul got the sharp knife and put it through the fish's spine. I am always surprised when a fish spurts blood. I turned away, as my stomach was still queasy, but the children watched closely, intently taking in this new sight.

And the whole scene was something. All around us the deep blue seas wore foamy white wave caps. To the west, a huge orange ball hung on the horizon, while overhead a slim new moon highlighted the two excited children, and the steel-blue and yellow fish, now flecked with brilliant red. But amidst all the excitement, Paul was noting that the wind was rising and the barometer was dropping. And when he got *Lorcha* under way again, he reefed a panel, and then another.

Late the following afternoon, I was lazily reading a book in the cockpit when there was a shout of surprise from Paul in the galley, "Fi, there's a freighter off our starboard beam."

I jumped guiltily and looked around the dodger. A large super-tanker was barely a mile away. Some lookout I was keeping.

"Why don't you call him for a fix and weather report," said Paul. "The barometer's still dropping and we may be in for a blow."

The motor vessel *Jerome*, registered in Liberia, was glad to talk with us.

"I've been watching you for some while," said the radio officer, "and wondering if you were going to call. What kind of rig is that anyway? It looks like a lug sail."

It turned out the radio officer was from England, and a small-boat sailor himself. We were surprised to learn that *Jerome* and her half cargo capacity of 67,000 tons of Nigerian crude oil had been "drifting" for two months, waiting for directions on where to deliver her spot market oil.

"Were you in the Cape Verdes?" I asked.

"Can't tell you anything about the port," said our new friend. "We were in Mindelo for only a few hours just to fuel up. But the weather's quite bad near the islands. The seas are up to twenty feet, the wind over thirty knots, and there's an awful lot of dust blown west from Africa. Take your sextant sights whenever you can because as you get farther south the dust will soon cover the sun."

We pinpointed our position on the chart, said farewell, and continued sailing south. Within three hours we had reefed the

100

sail another couple of panels. This was our fastest night of sailing to date, with *Lorcha* averaging six knots. It was not until the next night, however, that the waves reached the predicted twenty feet and we were once more down to two panels.

It was on my watch at 1:30 a.m. that the first of the bigger, breaking waves hit. I was actually watching the mounting wave pattern and formulating a fancy description in my mind, and even thinking about the odd larger waves that were rolling in from the east – all the way from Africa – when, whammy, a huge one from the east surged right over the cockpit from the stern quarter and cascaded down the main companionway, which I foolishly had left open.

Most of the water – and it looked like more than there actually was – was dumped right on poor, sleepy Penny, who was too astonished even to yell. I shouted for Paul to wake up and check her and change her bedclothes, while I pulled over the hatch cover and closed up the boat. A little late for the first wave, but there could be others.

At 4:30 a.m., on Paul's watch, another big easterner hit the port side with such force that Peter was knocked sideways out of his bunk and over the engine box. I hurriedly got up to get him back in bed and tuck him in further down the bunk where he would be protected by the narrow sides. He wasn't hurt and was sound asleep again in minutes.

The high waves with the odd one breaking continued the next morning and we kept Penny and Peter below. At nine o'clock I shouted "Land ho!" and we were pleased to see small mountains in the clouds about fifteen miles distant. A couple of hours later we could make out three distinct islands, but now there came the tricky part. Where was the fourth?

There are simply no distinguishing marks on the northern uninhabited side of the Cape Verdes – no towns, oil tanks, church spires, buildings, etc. São Vicente, the island we were heading for, should have been the second island from the west, with two islands lying east of her. But was our "missing" island located at the west or the east end of the group of three?

Closer and closer we sailed to the middle island, but still there was nothing to tell us which was the correct landfall. We were sailing nearer to land with some trepidation. The wind was strong enough for us to have only two panels of sail raised and we were headed for a lee shore. We had to get close enough to get our bearings – but not so close that we couldn't sail out again if we had to.

Paul was looking closely at the differing land heights.

"I think São Vicente might be the westernmost island we can see," he said. "I think we'll turn west and run downwind. I hope I'm right. It would be a hard sail back."

Paul disengaged the self-steering gear and we turned the boat west, Paul taking the tiller, while I strained to see what lay ahead. The children were still confined below decks. The wind was now behind us and the huge waves were surging under the stern. The boat was surfing down each crest, angling along the shore. We covered the nine-mile length of the island in record speed, with Paul worrying all the time about our possibly having to retrace our steps. Until suddenly – one minute it wasn't there, hidden by a freaky cloud of dust, and the next second a 6,000-foot-high mountain had popped up out of the haze right ahead of us. With São Antão identified, we now knew exactly where we were, and had time to look behind us.

The wind was now about forty knots, the waves had built up to twenty feet – and right behind us perhaps twenty dolphins were surfing merrily down the wave tops straight towards *Lorcha*. When we swooped down into the troughs between the waves, we had to look *up* to see the dolphins, who were actually above us. The water was so crystal-clear it was like looking through the glass of an aquarium, only much more vivid.

Although we were still afraid that one of the waves might fill the cockpit, we decided that we *had* to bring the kids up from below to see the dolphins.

Soon Peter and Penny, in life-jackets and safety harnesses, were in the cockpit, gaping in awe, first at the sleek golden dolphins and then at the hiss and roar of the giant waves as they passed underneath us.

More and more dolphins magically appeared, until there were

102

perhaps a hundred of them surging down the wave tops on each side of us. It was an incredible sight. For months after that, when one of the family mentioned dolphins, Penny would say, "Remember all the golden dolphins we saw near Mindelo?"

And Peter would add, "Yeah! And the waves, too."

What a way to be guided into harbour after a tough sail!

When the breakwater came in sight, we turned on our engine for the first time in eight days. Now *that's* cruising.

THE AFRICAN CAPE VERDES

13

The Cape Verde Islands were the first place we visited where the culture was truly different from our own. All the other islands we had visited so far had been primarily European in influence. Now we were in Africa – and Penny and Peter were fascinated.

They loved to go ashore just to "people-watch", and the colourful African markets were a favourite destination. Live animals squawked, clucked, bleated, and ran around the vibrantly dressed women who squatted over exotic fruit and vegetables spread around their feet. Everyone talked, chatted, shouted, and gestured – and the noise was deafening. At street corners, vendors sold spicy sausages or coconut sweetmeats from trays balanced atop their heads as they stood against a wall with one foot tucked up under the knee. The kids sampled everything, and soon Penny had bought a basket to balance on her head, and Peter was practising standing on one foot.

The heritage of the Cape Verdean is the black African slave and the European trader, usually Portuguese. The islands were uninhabited when one of Prince Henry's sailors discovered them in 1456, and Portuguese colonists began to arrive in 1462, soon bringing in slaves from West Africa. Now, five centuries later, people come in all colours here, but the major characteristics – the clothes, the houses, the markets – are undoubtedly African in influence.

104

And though the eight-island group was perhaps no poorer than many other parts of that great continent, it was – in our eyes at least – truly poverty-stricken. No doubt the deprivation had been intensified by the fact that the islands were in their twelfth year of drought. On the island of São Vicente, there had been no rainfall for fourteen years. Mud houses, thatched roofs, unshod feet, arid and deserted countryside, few roads – and an average annual per-capita income of $350. That was the Cape Verde Islands in 1984. And undaunted friendly people.

"You are the second Canadian yacht in Mindelo this year," said Teodoro Vierira, the head of the Mindelo Maritime Police. "Perhaps more yachts visit us than you realize. We had 225 altogether in 1983."

We were astounded. That's an awful lot of boats for a group of islands considered – at least in North America – to be somewhat off the beaten track.

There was a time, of course, when the Cape Verdes were very much *on* the beaten track. It was from there that Bartholomew Diaz, another of that incredible generation of Portuguese adventurers, set out in 1487 with two caravels and a store-ship in an attempt to find the end of the apparently endless African coast. After he had succeeded, rounding the Cape of Good Hope and establishing the prospect of a path to the Indies, Vasco da Gama came to finish the job in 1497. Da Gama spent a week in the Cape Verdes provisioning his ships before his epic two-year voyage to India and back established the route to the riches of the East.

105

After that, the route through the Cape Verdes became a Portuguese highway that by 1542 stretched as far as Japan. And only six months after da Gama's return, the Cape Verdes provided the launching-pad for another voyage, ostensibly to India. Thirty days out from the islands, Pedro Alvares Cabral was the first European to reach Brazil, claiming what proved to be a whole vast new land for Portugal.

And Brazil, of course, was to be *Lorcha's* next destination, after we had seen the Cape Verdes.

When we rowed ashore in Mindelo each day, there were always people on the beach willing to pull the boat in and tag along with us for the day. Some wanted a little money for their services. Other asked for old clothing, while most offered their services as friendly advisers and were content to see what, if anything, transpired.

Our particular friend in Mindelo was Ildo Duarte Rodriguez, who spoke English, but was an unlikely-looking guide with his ill-fitting trench coat, his shoeless, splayed feet, and his wild, curly black hair. Penny and Peter listened in fascination to his life story as we sat on the back of an open bouncing truck to visit a remote fishing village.

Twenty years earlier, Rodriguez had decided that the only way to better himself was to leave the Cape Verdes. And the only way he could see a poor boy from a large family getting away was on a ship. So he took to hanging around the harbour, and before long he had boarded a vessel bound for the United States – as a stowaway. (The children gasped.)

"I did it right," he said grinning. "I hid in the supply area. That way I did not have to see anyone or sneak about for food until the ship was well out at sea."

After five days, he announced himself. The captain made him work his passage to Baltimore, and then offered him a permanent job.

"First I had to see the Immigration people in Baltimore," recalled Ildo. "They were worried if I was being treated okay. They asked me, 'Do they give you enough food? Does the captain beat you?' "

106

"*Did* the captain beat you?" asked Peter, wide-eyed.

This was a more exciting story than *Treasure Island!*

In the last few years, the bigger ocean-going ships have stopped coming to the Cape Verdes, so Ildo's hard-won seaman's ticket is not of much use to him. Instead, he passes the days doing temporary work – and helping yachties like us see his islands. He told us his story in the course of a trip he organized (for us and another boat with children) to the remote fishing village of São Pedro. Probably the only visitors this village ever gets are from yachts.

It was a Sunday afternoon when we arrived and everyone was on the beach. A large net, towed out by fishermen in rowboats, was being laboriously hand-hauled on shore, with every able-bodied person helping – men, women, and children. It took about two hours to get the heavy net on land – and we all helped, of course – and if it was the day's catch, it was a poor one, with only a bucketful of small fish at the end of it all.

In times gone by when there was rain, it had been possible for the villagers to grow vegetables and other crops. Now the main diet was a mixture of imported maize and rice, flavoured with fish, when the catch was felicitous. But the people on the beach seemed an extraordinarily happy and close-knit community. Anyone with any French or English came up to speak with us, and it was a real eye-opener for Penny to be able to talk with the people who spoke in French. Soon she was happily running along the beach with a group of African children who were fascinated by her straight, light-coloured hair.

"I'm glad I'm learning French," she said later. "It's really good to be able to speak more than one language, isn't it?"

On another day, we took the early-morning ferry to the island of São Antão, the one that had been hidden in the dust on the day of our arrival. A local bus took us around the island and up and over the mountains to the other side. These roads had been built only recently and were all *hand-laid*. Their cobblestone paving wound in and out of the rugged contours, swooping through tunnels blasted through solid rock and climbing thousands of feet over the volcanic ridges. The man-hours necessary to lay them were unimaginable.

The dust, of course, was omnipresent, but we learned that even dust can have an interesting history. In 1832 the *Beagle*, with one Charles Darwin aboard as unpaid naturalist to the expedition, anchored in the Cape Verde Islands. There Darwin, the incorrigible collector, gathered and sent back to England specimens of dust brought by the wind from Africa. They contained no fewer than sixty-seven organic forms, all but two of them "inhabitants of fresh water". And here it was that Darwin saw shells embedded in a stratum of rock, which made him decide to investigate the world of geology further, and some day write a book about it.

A two-day sail is usually not much of a problem, except that it's tiring, but we weren't looking forward to our 170-mile sail from São Vicente southeast to São Tiago, because the seas were rough and the wind was gusting to fifty knots. There was no point in waiting hopefully for the moderate gale to abate. That's just how it was in January in the Cape Verdes.

The sail was memorable, however, because of Peter's sharp eyes. During the late afternoon of our second day at sea, when Paul was below, Penny, Peter, and I were having a discussion in the cockpit about eyesight. I am the only one in the family who is short-sighted. Everyone else has perfect vision, including old sharp-eyes Peter.

"I have such good eyes," Peter announced, "that I can even see a mountain over there."

He pointed south, where it would be impossible to see land.

Now Peter, like any four-year-old, is given to wild flights of fancy. We spot two whales and Peter sees ten. A flying fish lands on the deck – and Peter has them in his bunk.

"Yes, yes, Peter," I said, hardly glancing at the horizon.

Lorcha sailed on, and about half an hour later it was Paul's watch and I went below. Penny and Peter were still in the cockpit, and as soon as Paul had settled, Penny said casually, "Papa, Peter really does see a mountain, you know."

108

Paul looked in the direction she was pointing.

"Good lord," he shouted down the companionway. "There's a ruddy great mountain to starboard!"

Only the top of the 6,000-foot volcanic peak of the island of Fogo was visible as it reared high above the dense clouds on the horizon, almost looking like a sharp-pointed cloud itself.

It was a freak sighting, as visibility was down to three or four miles in the dust. According to our DR, we should have been about forty-five miles from Fogo. Yet here it was, an estimated fifteen miles away. The wayward Canaries current had swept us off course by thirty miles in thirty hours. But for Peter's sighting of Fogo, we would have sailed right past São Tiago – with the next stop Brazil, a passage for which we were not yet prepared.

We altered course, suitably thanking our toddling navigator.

When we rowed ashore and tied our dinghy to the rocks in Praia, a group of young teenagers, some of whom spoke English, were hanging around the beaching area to meet us. They were mostly kids who couldn't afford the $2.40 cents a month it takes to go to high school. They'd show us the town, carry groceries, and help us with drinking-water. They were polite and helpful and asked only a few pennies for their services. A visit to your boat is considered a great treat.

But none of them had heard of Damasio Mendes Tuaures, the weaver. We had heard that the last living Master Weaver in the Cape Verdes lived on São Tiago. Hand-woven cloth has always been held in high regard in the Cape Verdes, and the traditionally woven blue-and-white material was actually the unit of currency in the seventeenth century. Cape Verdean cloth was prized all over Europe, and thirty of the six-panelled "panos" was the price of a slave.

In Europe or North America, everyone would know of a famous artist living in their area, and if he was a "master artist", tourists would be beating a well-worn track to his house to see him actually working. But it took us four days of intensive work to find Damasio Mendes Tuaures. In fact, it took the combined efforts of René Tourigay, the Canadian representative from the

United Nations Development Projects, Peggy Yates, the wife of the American Ambassador to the Cape Verdes, Bato Badolfo, a Field Consultant from the United States Agency for International Development, and a small boy on the beach, to get us to Tuaures, while Penny and Peter stayed at the Embassy.

In due course Peggy, Bato, Paul, and I were in Ribeiro São Miguel, the first green valley we had seen in São Tiago. The big job here, and the one Bato was in charge of, was water conservation and the introduction of new crops. Though the river valley itself was completely dry (three rainfalls in 1983), Bato and a team of workers were harnessing underground water in deep wells dug behind earthen dams, all built by hand. Now, only two years since Badolfo's team had started work, water in the wells was lasting ten months of the year – this in an area that formerly had water for perhaps eight weeks.

When there is a rainfall, it can cause a flash flood on the hard-packed dry river bed, and the road through the valley had been washed out. Only sturdy jeeps like ours could make their way through, and our progress was slow, but interesting. When farmers wanted to show us their crops, we all got down to inspect them and give encouragement. The 12-kilometre journey took us about an hour, but at last we were at the end of the road.

"Here's where we start climbing," said Bato cheerfully, hopping out of his jeep.

The mountain seemed almost vertical, but a rough path zigzagged its way up. About an hour of hard climbing later we reached our goal, a ramshackle lean-to outside a small stone house, with two men sitting at ancient weaving looms. They must have been watching us for at least an hour as the valley lay spread before them as they worked, but they courteously got up and greeted us warmly. We had found our Master Weaver and his colleague.

With Bato acting as interpreter, we learned that Tuaures had been a weaver all his life, following in the footsteps of his father before him. The looms were obviously old – heir-looms, you might say. The threads were shifted by shaped branches connected by cords to other sticks under the men's feet, with the cotton held taut about fifteen feet away by a huge stone. Cottage industry at its most primitive.

But the material and the intricate designs were lovely. There were about half a dozen different patterns one could choose from, based on ancient patterns, with some new ideas introduced. The most striking material, however, was the traditional dark-blue-and-white cloth, still woven in the traditional narrow-panelled strips by these "modern" weavers. The panels were then sewn together in strips of six, producing a 2-metre length of material, which could then be made into anything the wearer wanted. The local custom was to wear it decoratively round one's waist, where money and small purchases could be safely laid in its soft folds. Both Peggy and I ordered a length of material in hand-dyed deep-blue indigo.

We saw no one wearing the traditional cloths in "sophisticated" Praia, but when we visited the interior market town of Assomada high in the mountains, many Cape Verdean women were still wearing them. We saw both newly woven and old cloths in this bustling market, and created quite a stir when we offered to buy an old cloth from a woman wearing one. She fairly tore it from her waist to sell it to us, everyone crowding round to watch the unusual transaction.

Meanwhile, back at the American Embassy, Penny and Peter were having a great day. The Embassy servants, missing the five Yates children, who were all back in school in the States, were making quite a fuss of our two little ones and had been baking cookies for them all day. When the inestimable John Yates returned to his house for lunch at midday, his guests at the impressive Residence table, formally set for three, were none other than our two youngsters!

I am afraid it wasn't the company that impressed our kids most.

"The greatest thing about the Embassy," said Peter, with round eyes, "is that you have TWO desserts for lunch – cake *and* cookies!"

FEAR AT SEA

14

"Aren't you ever frightened?" many of our friends ask, thinking of the strong winds and high waves we encounter. The answer so far is, "Not really." We have been in gale-force winds several times and in a number of tough situations with heavy seas. But we have never been really frightened, though leaving port for any ocean crossing – especially the first one – can cause acute anxiety. No matter how many coastal passages of a few hundred miles you may have done, secure in the knowledge that land is somewhere just under the horizon, and that the world is not flat, and yachts do not fall off the edge of it, you are aware that an ocean crossing is different. With the land falling behind and a fair wind, it's easy to start thinking that it could be difficult or impossible to return.

Before our first passage, from St. John's to the Azores, we fussed and picked, doing a myriad of detailed projects which perhaps added to our mental preparedness, but which probably added little to our safety or well-being at sea. Lashings on the dinghy were doubled and tripled in case we encountered the ultimate storm – and then I worried about whether I would be able to free the dinghy quickly enough if there was an emergency. I fretted about the placement of the life raft – and then worried about whether it was securely enough attached or not. We brought on extra

112

Leaving Praia . . . Ocean Passages for the World . . .
the doldrums . . . freighter threat . . . underwater mystery . . .
strange light . . . crossing the equator . . . sharks . . . intertropical
convergence zone

---

jerry cans of fuel and water, only adding to our weight and perhaps even slowing us down.

To date, we have found that ocean crossings are mostly fun and interesting. The colour of the sea changes with the moods of the weather, which has to be taken as it comes. We have never been able to get weather forecasts once out of sight of land except occasionally from a passing ship. (And in that first crossing, the first freighter I asked for a forecast produced the heart-stopping reply, "Would you like the report on the hurricane first?" It was far to the south, and I recovered.)

Yet after a few days at sea a rhythm develops where small observations take on new meaning. A change in the motion of the boat may mean a change in wind strength. An ocean swell from a new direction is probably bringing new winds. Different cloud formations help foretell various weather patterns. It is fascinating to find all our senses becoming more keenly attuned to nature as we study the world around us.

The sky is a big bowl overhead, across which the sun and clouds march every day. After sunset the sky is a wonder only to be fully appreciated on lonely nightwatches at sea. The stars swirl around Polaris, changing positions in a seemingly mysterious manner, while watching the moon rising late at night can be an equally puzzling and mesmerizing experience. At first you cannot figure out why the sky is lightening on the horizon. Distant clouds mask its shape, which you imagine to be anything from a far-off fishing boat to a UFO. But gradually the shape and identity become clearer, and you relax again and regain your confidence. And you realize why the ancient people held the moon in special regard.

But for all our confidence and care, strange and inexplicable things can happen far from land, and they do tend to get the adrenalin going. It is then that you are most aware of your remoteness and your vulnerability. You know that, regardless of what happens, you are on your own.

On our longest passage to date, about 1,500 miles from the Cape Verde Islands to Brazil, we had two such occasions. They gave Fiona and me pause for thought, though neither or them disturbed Penny or Peter a bit. In fact, they thought both incidents a bit of a lark, and merely interesting enough to fill the monotony of the day!

All twelve yachts that had been at anchor in Praia when we arrived had left, so there were no more goodbyes to say as we sailed southwest with only three panels of sail up in the gusty thirty-knot wind. We were both sad and happy to leave Praia – sad because we had really enjoyed our four-week stay in the Cape Verdes, but glad to be leaving the dry, barren landscape and the fine red dust that permeated everything. The dust, in fact, remained with us until our ninth day out near the equator, when rain squalls washed the air clean.

We would be sailing across the equator into the South Atlantic ocean. On the way, we knew we would pass through the doldrums, the area where the northeast trade winds and the clockwise circuit of currents of the North Atlantic mix with the counter-clockwise currents and southeast trade winds of the South Atlantic ocean. It is an area noted for its calms and its rain squalls.

Authors such as Joseph Conrad and Herman Melville wrote of the old sailing ships lying becalmed for weeks or even months in this area, and about the sailors of old throwing buckets of water on their cotton sails to help catch the wind. Sailing-ship crews would lower their boats onto the glassy sea and, with men fainting from heat exhaustion, they would row for days or weeks trying to tow the mother ship through the calms. "Crossing the line under an ash wind" was the wonderfully romantic phrase used

114

by sailing masters to describe this sort of passage. It meant cross-ing the equator with the sailors pulling on their ash-wood oars.

When crossing from Praia (15°N, 23°30'W) to the Brazilian island of Fernando de Noronha (3°40'S, 32°20'W), we followed the sailing directions in the British Admiralty publication *Ocean Passages for the World*, a compendium of advised sailing routes around the world, compiled by the experts who circled the globe for commerce in the golden age of sail. First published in 1895, it is still considered an essential reference book by today's modern sailor.

In its introductory remarks, the book states

> It must be stressed, however, that the routing advice . . . was originally intended for large sailing vessels able to stand up to, and take advantage of, heavy weather to be expected on many of the passages . . . by a well-found vessel of about 2,000 tons, which in good conditions, could log speeds of 10 to 12 knots. . . .

Lorcha's tonnage is 7.19, and her average passage speed is only four knots. Yet I religiously followed the advice given by those sailing masters of yesteryear, as I do on most passages.

The doldrums officially cover an area from 5°N to 5°S. The inter-tropical convergence zone is the dead-flat band that enlarges and contracts and even meanders within the doldrums. This is the area where the barometric pressure never varies, the ocean has long, glassy swells, and sailing ships lie dead in the water. Another com-plicating factor is the harmatan winds which blow off the Sahara Desert. During the months of January and February, the fine red dust blown off the barrens of central Africa is picked up by the northeast trade winds. Because of the dust, visibility can be limited to two or three miles for up to one thousand miles from Africa's west coast. With the sun appearing as a fuzzy ball in the clouds, sextant sights can be difficult to take, and of questionable accuracy.

By day three, the winds lessened to a pleasant fifteen knots, and for the first time in three months we had full sail up.

By the fifth day, the winds were falling off and were now about eight knots. It was slow but comfortable sailing, with our distance covered down to about eighty miles a day. This was, in fact, the first ocean passage during which Fiona and Penny were able to do some schoolwork.

But it was hot! We decided to give the children a treat by rigging a plastic sheet in the footwell of the cockpit and filling it with sea water for a cooling bath. All the floating toys joined Peter and Penny, and they shouted and laughed all afternoon. Water play! Why didn't we think of it earlier!

A distant twinkle on the horizon early in the evening put us in touch with the friendly Soviet freighter *Marshal Budenny*, whose radio officer had spent three years in Quebec. He cheerfully verified our position.

On our sixth day, we were well into the doldrums, but though the wind was light, we were still sailing steadily. In the evening we sailed through a large school of tuna, who put on a spectacular display of jumping and turning in the air beside the boat as they fed, quite enthralling the children.

So far the passage had been relaxed and almost idyllic. Our first strange experience started the following afternoon. I was on watch, lounging casually in the cockpit, and Fiona was napping below. The dust was still around us, with visibility down to three miles, when I looked up to see a large motor vessel about two miles astern. I should have seen him earlier.

"Is the VHF on?" I called down to Fiona. "There's a big freighter coming up behind us."

As soon as the radio was switched on, we heard the tail end of a message in a thick foreign accent:

". . . I do not get out of the way of anybody. I do not get out of the way of anybody. . . . "

We were the only two vessels in sight, and this huge many-thousand-ton monster was right on our course and closing fast. As if to underscore his statement, his ship's horn blew four blasts, the signal to "get out of my way". To say we were stunned was to put it mildly.

"Is he threatening us?" asked Fiona in disbelief as she grabbed the microphone.

"This is the Canadian sailing yacht *Lorcha* acknowledging a

116

motor vessel two miles astern. We understand you do not give way to other vessels. We are altering course to get out of your path. Please identify yourself. Over."

The boat replied she was the Soviet salvage vessel *Geophysic*. Then added,

"Keep well clear. I do not keep out of the way of small ships."

There was no mistaking his words. Fiona took them down in shorthand. She was now very angry.

"This is the sailing vessel *Lorcha*. We would remind the captain of *Geophysic* that ships of all countries sail in international waters and respect the right of other vessels to be there. All ships obey the international regulations for the prevention of collision of vessels at sea. In the interests of safety, we have altered course twenty degrees. Please pass on our starboard side."

International regulations clearly state, of course, that, except for ships in restricted waters, power vessels keep clear of sailing vessels. We had right of way, but you have to use common sense when a very small, manoeuvrable ship is dealing with a very large power vessel. You can't always demand your rights, or you may be dead right – right and dead. Fiona wisely didn't waste time pointing out we had "right of way" to this boat.

But if she wasn't going to argue about the vessel's physical actions, she was not prepared to let him go without an explanation, and she had him spell out the name and port of registry to make sure we got them right. After this, the Russian vessel abruptly added, "Now we are saying goodbye."

"She's well clear now," I shouted down the companionway. "But I can see she's towing something underwater."

"*Geophysic*, what are you towing?" demanded Fiona imperiously. There was radio silence.

Fiona, not one to give up, kept calling. (I was almost beginning to feel sorry for our adversary.) In the end, *Geophysic* did come back on the air, not to give what Fiona had asked, but to confirm our position.

Then, "My English is not so good," said the operator. "Goodbye. . . . "

Whatever it was, we were not about to be told, and her

underwater secret disappeared into the haze with her. Our adrenalin slowly got back to normal as we surveyed the empty and non-threatening seas around us. . . .

We were glad to be able to relax under light airs the next day. The boat was going so slowly, though still under sail, that we noticed we had picked up two friends. Two stunningly beautiful dorado – flashing green, yellow, and turquoise – were swimming alongside, darting in and out of the shade of the hull. We had already hauled in a skipjack tuna for supper, so we didn't think of catching them, but simply enjoyed watching them, first at the bow and then at the stern and sometimes just lazing alongside. They made no attempt to hide as Penny and Peter hung over the sides to peer at them.

There was much clanging and clattering of the sail overnight as the boat rolled in the swell with only light winds to push her, but we thought we would keep sailing as long as we could. The light airs were understandable as we were now well into the doldrums, where to be under sail at all was a pleasant surprise.

With the boat speed now down to one lousy knot, we turned on the engine. It was our ninth day, and the first time we had touched the helm. We motored the remainder of the day and all night, turning the engine off at nine o'clock the following morning to have a late breakfast in peace. By the time we had finished and cleared up, a light breeze had sprung up.

We hoisted sail. Where we had expected to be motoring for days, we were sailing again at two and a half knots.

There were rain squalls on the horizon around us, which were very welcome, as they washed the fine red dust that had plagued us for so long out of the air. The seas were flat and there were no birds or sea life around us, but we were all excited because we would be crossing the equator that night.

"Crossing the equator at night? We won't be able to see anything," grumbled Penny and Peter.

"There's nothing to see anyway," I laughed. "But you can mark it off on our chart tomorrow."

118

But I was wrong. It was Fiona's watch, and just before we crossed the equator she saw a stationary white flashing light at about 0°05'N, 27°50'W.

It was, of course, impossible. We were slap in the middle of the Atlantic. The nearest land was the St. Peter and St. Paul Rocks, but they were a few hundred miles from us, and they were unlit.

Fiona watched the light for about thirty long minutes, establishing beyond doubt that the bright light was flashing every four seconds. Then she woke me.

"I got quite a shock when I saw it," she said when I came up on deck. "It's impossible – and yet there it is."

The light flashed steadily on our port side.

After several days at sea with only small x's on the chart to give an indication where you are, you can become disoriented, doubting your navigation. What was a light that for all the world looked like a coastal light-house doing flashing at us when we were, literally, in the middle of nowhere? The fact that the night was very black with no moon didn't help our confused feelings.

Were we where we thought we were? Was this some recently discovered hazard to navigation not yet noted on the chart? Could it be a distress signal? A flashing light on the life raft of some shipwrecked mariners?

One by one we went through the possibilities. All of them led us nowhere. We tried calling on the vhf, but received no reply.

"Perhaps it's the buoy that marks the equator," I joked, trying to lighten our sombre mood.

We satisfied ourselves as well as we could that it was not a distress signal, since it was too bright and consistent to be the light of a bobbing raft. We sailed on until at last it disappeared over the horizon, about four hours later ... leaving us wondering, wondering ...

We had light-heartedly discussed the possibilities of properly celebrating crossing the equator. Should I dress as King Neptune before the children awoke and splash them with South Atlantic brine as they came out into the cockpit? Should we have a treat and toot the horn to make frightening noises to ward off the evil spirits and beasties of the Southern Ocean?

Because it was quite calm, with little wind and flat seas, Fi thought the special event should be marked by a quick dip in the sea and a swim round the boat. But I was reluctant to allow anyone overboard in mid-ocean, though one does often hear of others jumping in for a swim when the boat is becalmed far from land.

"I'd really rather you didn't go overboard," I said. But Fiona was still looking at the cool water with a rather longing eye when Penny, who was standing at the stern of the boat, gave a yell.

"Come and look at this big fish," she shouted.

There nibbling gently on our rudder was a six-foot-long white-tipped shark. He turned and eyed us from beside the boat, not a whit distracted by all the attention he was getting.

I couldn't resist it.

"Still want to go swimming, sweetheart?" I asked Fiona.

I pulled in the trailing log line as another shark swam up to bump its nose against the spinner as if to bite a fishing lure. Two more sharks swam up to linger just under our transom as we lined the pushpit peering down at their distinctive fins poking out of the water within arm's reach. There were soon perhaps a dozen more, one much larger than the rest.

We watched them with a mixture of fascination and dread, Peter a little more apprehensive than the rest of us. He too peered over the edge of the boat, but he kept a tight hold of Fiona's hand and he wasn't as full of questions as usual. After about an hour the sharks suddenly came together and shot off to the west.

"Perhaps they've heard of another yacht crossing – and want to see if the crew are silly enough to swim," I said, unable to resist a further dig.

Next day we were truly in the intertropical convergence zone. The sea was flat, with light swells rolling us in every direction.

A huge freighter on the busy St. Lawrence Seaway (top) provides a contrast with *Lorcha* and a larger American yacht in the tiny harbour at Flores, the westernmost island in the Azores.

Not laundry but shark meat hanging on a line attracts Paul's attention near the village of Lobos in mountainous Madeira.

The busy harbour of Las Palmas in the Canary Islands proves to be a great place for Peter and Penny to make new friends.

On the Cape Verdes (at this time in their twelfth year of drought) dust blows over from the Sahara, and water is a precious resource. By contrast (below) there is no shortage of water in the green depths of the Amazon jungle, as the family is taken by canoe up-river from Manaus.

In the Amazon there is a belief that a Victoria Regis lily pad will hold the weight of a five year old. Here a delighted Peter tests the theory.

On the wide – and muddy – Amazon, with the port of Belém in the distance.

In French Guiana the family spent a night on the beach to watch the giant Luth turtles come ashore to lay their eggs. Here a turtle makes its way back to the sea, watched over by Penny and Peter.

In Isla Marguarita a Venezuelan visitor to *Lorcha* shows Fiona how to make cornmeal arepas.

In Bonaire, in the Netherlands Antilles, the remarkable Dee Scarr introduces Fiona to some underwater friends.

The clear waters around Bonaire teem with fish so tame and unafraid that they will feed from your hands. Here Paul, Peter, and Penny investigate the reefs.

Peter and Paul admire a fresh-caught dorado, and think about dinner.

Birthdays are all-important on the boat. Here Peter, Paul, and Penny cut out chocolate boat shapes for Penny's seventh birthday, and think about dinner.

Still all in the same boat!

The wind puffed fitfully from every point of the compass and several rain squalls drenched us. We motored through the day, but in the early evening we began to feel a light breeze from the southeast.

Luck and the southeast trades were with us ... and on our twelfth night at sea, we sighted the strong flashing light on Fernando de Noronha. We reefed the sail to slow down. By the light of the full moon we rounded the rocky islets off the east end of the main island, to anchor at dawn among six other yachts in the Bay of São Antão. We were in South America.

It had been a comfortable passage, but typical?

We have learned that the only typical thing about ocean passages is that they are all different. And they all have their surprises.

NOT IN THE
CURRICULUM

15

We're of two minds about the education of our children.

Are they missing out on their academic learning because they're not in the formal school system? Will they be able to fit in with their peers when they do eventually return to a shore-based life? Or is this protracted family voyaging of ours giving them a better grounding and experience of life than they could ever have in the normal city educational process?

One thing is for sure: both children's experiences are way beyond the normal school curriculum. . . .

"Papa," asks Peter, "when will we get to harbour?"

"A few more hours," I tell him. "See that land over there?"

"Is that an island or a country?" he asks very seriously.

Explaining world geography to a small boy of intense curiosity can be quite baffling for a parent.

After we left Canada, we visited many islands along the eastern side of the Atlantic Ocean. Every port was on an island and usually each new port was in a different country. Peter thought he understood. You sail to islands on boats.

But when we sailed across the equator to the small Brazilian island of Fernando de Noronha, he began to get confused. This was Brazil, just another small island.

Islands and continents . . . heavy surf . . . overturned dinghy . . .
seeing in the dark

"Not quite," I explained patiently. "This little island is only part of Brazil, not the whole country."

I explained we would soon be sailing to mainland Brazil and that we would no longer be travelling among islands, but along the large country of Brazil.

"Brazil is not on an island but on a continent," I told him. "And that continent has many other countries on it."

"A continent?" asked Peter, stumbling over the unfamiliar word. "But is that like an island?"

I got out the world atlas and showed him our route.

"See all these small spots on this map," I said. "Those are islands. See how small they are. They are surrounded by water, well away from any other land. This is Brazil, a very large country attached to other countries."

We read off the names of several countries on the South American continent, talking about the ones we would visit, and the various ports along the way. How sometimes we would sail along the coast, while at others we would cross bodies of water to get to a new place.

But Peter was still thinking.

"Is South America an island?" he asked. "It's surrounded by water."

Well, in truth, I had to admit it is nearly surrounded by water, except for a small bit that attaches it to Central and North America.

"Some continents are attached to each other," I explained. "Like the Americas or Europe or Asia. But others can be separate. Australia is both a continent and an island. That's because it's so big."

123

"But," said our tenacious youngster, "it's only one country, just like a small island. . . ."

This was a practical exercise in geography, spawned by a child's need to know something about the many places he was visiting, trying to understand about the world around him.

It was not the time to launch into an explanation of continental land masses, coastlines, and island groups, and their juxtapositions. Besides, another new harbour was looming up. I decided to sidestep the geography lesson, freeing the anchor, clearing the windlass, getting out the detailed charts, and making all of the other preparations that are routine when closing with land.

"What's important?" I asked. "Shall we discuss whether we're coming to an island or a continent – or whether we'll find any ice-cold milk when we get to town?"

"Milk," said Peter immediately. "How long before we get into harbour?"

There are some things that we would prefer the children did not have to experience – though as long as a dangerous situation works out all right in the end, I suppose it's a lesson well learned, for children have to learn to cope with difficult situations somewhere along the line.

Penny and Peter met with one such situation in Fernando de Noronha, where getting ashore was a real problem. The anchorage is open to the north and west, and, though it's protected from the southeast trade winds, a heavy surf pounds the beach. When we arrived, we had to negotiate our first dinghy landing in surf.

We eyed the breaking water in front of the fishing station, where the yacht dinghies seemed to land. Was there a pattern to the waves? Did any one landing-place look better than another? Was the wave height affected by the tide? We saw other yachties try to land, arriving ashore in varying degrees of wetness.

A fishing boat came in. We waited to see how the locals passed through the surf. They tied their boat to its offshore mooring and threw their morning's catch into a small rowboat; then the four men headed for shore. As they neared the surf, all four leapt into the water, and with one man clutching either side of the bow and the other two at the stern, weighing it down, they swam the boat to the beach. They were taking no chances on losing their catch!

Thus forewarned, we put the children into their life-jackets, wrapped the camera, ship's papers, and money in several layers of plastic, and put the valuables in a knapsack on Fiona's back. I tied the oars, seat, and bailer to the dinghy so they couldn't be lost and started to row for shore, pausing just outside the breakers to watch the wave pattern. Some yachtsmen ashore waved to us to pull hard between the heavier swells. I looked about, hesitated in order to take a quick look at the shore, and then pulled as fast as I could, hoping to land before the next big breakers overtook us.

But the hesitation had been too long. About 20 metres from the beach, a large wave began to lift us and I knew we were gone. As the wave curled, the dinghy spun sideways, began to fill with water, and then flipped over.

When the roar of the surf receded and I surfaced, I found myself half under the overturned dinghy in about 1.5 metres of water. A quick look around showed that Penny and Fiona had been thrown clear. But . . .

"Where's Peter?" yelled Fiona. She dived under the dinghy, I swam after her, and there, in the dinghy's air pocket, was Peter hanging on wide-eyed inside, not sure whether to laugh or cry.

"Take a breath and we'll swim out from under," said Fiona, taking Peter's hand. I set about righting our small vessel, and we soon gathered our floating belongings, sat our four-year-old in the swamped dinghy, and waded ashore to where Penny was waiting.

"Well, that was sure an adventure," said Fiona cheerily. "Peter, you did just the right thing staying with the boat."

Peter's little face cleared and colour came flooding back.

"Was I very brave, Mama?" he asked.

"You certainly were," said Fiona as she hugged both children to reassure them again.

"I was just swimming to shore," said Penny carelessly, terribly pleased with herself for this display of independence.

At least this lesson had turned out well.

We were sitting in the cockpit one day with the self-steering gear handling the boat when Peter started a serious discussion.

"Can you see further in the day or at night?" he asked.

The answer was pretty obvious to me.

"You can see much further in daylight," I replied. "Darkness sort of hems things in. That's why I always like to cook supper before it gets too dark. You can see what you're eating better."

There was a long silence, and then

"How far away are the stars?" asked Peter.

I fell into it.

"Millions of miles," I answered absently. "Even the closest ones are very far away."

"If you can see further in daylight," said Peter patiently, "then how come you can see those stars which are millions of miles away at night?"

There is no doubt that voyaging is opening the eyes of our children to the world around them, and broadening their horizons in every way. And we're learning along with them. . . .

DOLPHIN
DELIGHTS

16

Nothing brings Penny and Peter on deck as fast as the cry of "Dolphins at the bow". For who can resist these sleek, streamlined marine mammals as they roll and perform in the bow wave. With what looks like a permanent smile on their faces, they seem to be having so much fun as they swoop about, pausing now and then to come up close to watch the watchers!

Armed with Erich Hoyt's *The Whale Watchers' Handbook*, which identifies thirty-seven different species, Penny and Peter eagerly watch our visitors and then plunge below decks to thumb through the pages to try to identify the species of animals they have been seeing. Not always an easy task.

We whetted their appetites with *Nine True Dolphin Stories* by Margaret Davidson to help the children understand these friendly small cetacea who roam the oceans of the world.

The stories are rather amazing – Pelorus Jack, who escorted ships through New Zealand's Cook Strait for twenty-two years; Opo, named after the town of Opononi, New Zealand, who became so friendly with the townspeople she would swim between the children's legs and take them for a ride on her back; and Atlantic Zippy, who let herself be blindfolded so scientists could prove she could find objects through sound waves instead of sight.

All cruising yachts have special stories to relate

"Dolphins at the bow" . . . amazing stories . . . dawn acrobatics . . . breeding-grounds . . . swimming with the dolphins . . . command performance . . . night-time artists' trails

---

about encounters with dolphins, and ours, of course, include the amazing dolphin escort into the Cape Verdes in seas so high that we could look up at the dolphins in the waves behind us. But that was nothing compared to our experience at Fernando de Noronha, our first landfall in Brazil and the South Atlantic. Its strategic position about two hundred miles off the northeast corner of Brazil had made it a natural spot for pirates, and the children kept a sharp lookout for a skull-and-crossbones flag until we reminded them that it was a pirate stronghold only in the sixteenth and seventeenth centuries. The pirates were run out of town in 1738 by the Portuguese, who were tired of having their sailing ships plundered. Then they built Forte dos Remedios, a town and a prison for any pirates foolish enough to return to the island. We wouldn't see any pirates, but the ruins of the old prison still stand.

But much more important than any ruined prison was the wildlife around us. Booby and frigate birds wheeled overhead and green sea turtles popped their heads out of the waves to eye us as we lay at anchor, but . . .

"Have you ever seen so many dolphins?" we shouted to one another.

There were thousands swimming among the six yachts anchored in the Bay of São Antão. The island is a major breeding-ground for the bottlenose and spinner dolphins, and they displayed no fear of people or boats visiting their territory. You could literally lean over the side and stroke their backs as their curiosity brought them close to the hull.

"I touched one. I touched one," yelled Peter as he lay flat on the deck, so precariously balanced he threatened to fall over any minute.

"Look at the babies. Look at the babies," shouted Penny as tiny little white ones were guided up to the surface by the adults, looking for all the world as if they were showing *their* infants what *our* children looked like.

We watched in amazement as other yachties plunged into the water to swim with the dolphins, who almost touched the swimmers' noses as they peered into their swimming-masks. They were clearly as interested in the swimmers as the swimmers were in them, and dolphin language ("Hey, come and look at this fat human!") echoed through the water in high-pitched squeaks and pings. Sometimes out of sheer high spirits one would leap its full length straight out of the water, often doing a spiralling turn before plunging back in. Others lay belly to belly in the water as they mated.

All this was a charming and wondrous experience for all of us, especially since it all took place at the main anchorage where the yachts and four local fishing boats anchored. We soon learned that though the dolphins sometimes visited this anchorage, especially when a new yacht arrived, their real home and breeding-grounds were just down the coast at Dolphin Bay. Yachts were not allowed to anchor in the bay, which was surrounded by impenetrable cliffs overgrown with tropical vegetation that protected it from the shore side. But yachts were allowed to sail in for a few hours of daylight, provided the dolphins were not molested.

Several days later we slowly sailed down the leeward side of the island to explore the bay, for Penny and Peter would never have allowed us to sail away without a visit.

"I can't see any dolphins," pouted Peter, brows together as he stood on lookout at the bow.

I motorsailed slowly towards the cliffs, which seemed to plunge straight into the water – and suddenly the dolphins were all around us. Dozens, scores, hundreds of dolphins.

"Papa, can we go in swimming with them?" asked Penny anxiously.

I didn't see why not, as we had seen lots of adults do so. So, with the children in life-jackets, Fiona, Penny, and Peter jumped into the water while I let the boat drift with the engine in neutral.

"You can really hear them 'talking'," Penny called excitedly as she came up from another underwater visit. She and Peter were laughing and shouting happily, churning the water as they tried to play with the sleek and frisky creatures around them. Fiona, meanwhile, was content to tread water nearby, keeping an eye on the excited children but at the same time obviously enjoying the experience, too.

We could see the dolphins swimming through the wonderfully clear water at least 20 metres away. They would often come surging up from below the two children, only to swerve away from them at the last minute to perform some of their acrobatics, much to the squeals of delight from our two waterbabies. After a "performance", the dolphins would turn back almost as if to check that Penny and Peter had been watching, and to see what they thought.

After half an hour, *Lorcha*'s crew climbed reluctantly back on board.

"Mummy, I can't believe they let you come up to them like that," said Penny, shivering. "Oh, I wish I could understand what they were saying."

The two children sat in the sun to warm up and continued to watch their fascinating friends with unswerving concentration until late in the afternoon, when we sailed back to the Bay of São Antão to anchor overnight.

Peter was never able to forget this experience, and dolphins remain his favourite animal. To this day, both Penny and Peter collect pictures, photos, and dolphin toys, and will read any book or newspaper article on the subject.

Though we have since seen many dolphins, we have never again experienced them in such abundance or in such carefree abandon.

There are times at sea when Penny gets up in the middle of the night to see the stars and to watch for constellations to rise above the horizon so she can check them off in her stars and planets book. An added bonus is a night-time dolphin visitation. On a moonless night, especially if we are sailing through an area rich in phosphorescent plankton, the dark sea, reflecting only the starlight and producing its own sparkles, seems to merge with the sky. It can be very black and very quiet, until . . .

A loud, sometimes startling, hoarse gasp is heard. It is the cry of a dolphin breaching next to *Lorcha* for his required breath of air. And Penny and I leap to the side of the boat to watch.

The trails of brightly lit phosphorescence follow the dolphin like jet streams following an aeroplane. The glittering track leads under the keel, then to a leap at the bow, or perhaps through several circular whorls and splashes of light as a few friendly creatures leap in synchronization with a wave slapping *Lorcha's* hull.

These nocturnal visits by dolphins are in some ways even more thrilling than their daytime frolics. For the whirling lines and cascades of brilliant moving streaks can be more complex and intricate than any artist's palette. And yet, despite all the activity, we never see the actual creature in the dark, following only his magnificent and always moving trail.

It is one of those slightly scary and unanticipated thrills that are always a delight to share with one's children. And it is one that is only possible to experience when ocean-voyaging.

BRAZILIAN
PROBLEMS

17

The easternmost bulge of South America is an area known for its miles of palm-fringed beaches, small fishing villages, and the sailing fishing rafts called jangadas. It is also known for its drought and poverty.

But Brazil, originally inhabited by the Tupi-Guarani Indians, and discovered for the Portuguese by Cabral's voyage from the Cape Verdes in 1500, has had its moments of prosperity. The focus of exports over the centuries has swung from sugar to coffee to the rubber boom and then to gold and minerals. The country has never, however, managed to sustain its economy for any length of time, owing (according to the Brazilian writer Holanda) to a continuous and strong desire for quick wealth and for "collecting the fruit without planting the tree".

It is also known for its bureaucratic fussiness, as we were to discover when we registered at the Natal Yacht Club, our first port on mainland Brazil, and asked what paperwork was necessary here. We discovered that the paperwork for our little yacht was the same as for cargo ships – and there's plenty of it.

The islands we had previously visited were relatively easy to check in and out of, but Brazil was to establish a pattern we encountered over and over again as we travelled northwest up the South American coast. In most of these countries the harbour officials addressed me as "Captain Howard" or just "Captain". This is meant as a symbol of respect for having piloted a ship, however small, over many ocean miles. In return, I was expected to address officials in a similar respectful manner, and to dress accordingly. The plain facts are that in poor countries, people with shabby clothes, barefoot, and with unkempt hair are often ignored, disdained, or taken advantage of by government officials. Scruffily dressed yachtsmen get the same treatment.

That morning I washed, shaved, brushed my hair, and put on long trousers, a dress shirt, and socks along with my shoes. Fiona put on a skirt, as women should not visit officials wearing shorts.

At the Port Captain's office, we reported arrival time and provided such details as registered name, port and number, length, draft, tonnage, cargo, passengers, and three prepared crew lists giving name, nationality, passport number, and expiry date, as well as the date of birth of each person on board. Naturally we had with us our official clearance from our last port, which confirmed details of our vessel and crew and reported that we had left the country in good grace and with no harbour charges outstanding.

Brazil was the first country we had visited for which a health certificate was required, and we all had to visit the port doctor. He certified that we were in good health, had had no contact with any serious communicable diseases, and had had the required shots as noted in our International Certificate of Vaccination. He filled in a form to be presented to the immigration office.

A visit to the customs office was necessary to receive permission for the boat and its equipment to stay in the country for a prescribed time before import duty was due. This period is usually anywhere from six months to one year. The customs office wanted a detailed list of how much alcohol, tobacco, guns, ammunition, etc., we had on board. They also required a list of ship's equipment for such things as radios, camera, sextant, SatNav, binoculars, compass, and any other goods they feared we might try to sell while in the country. Brazil allowed yachts to keep their firearms and ammunition on board while in their territorial waters. (Many other countries confiscate guns, returning the equipment only after the final clearance papers are obtained.)

The immigration department was our last call, and there we presented the fat pile of all the papers obtained from the preceding offices. This time we filled in forms detailing our date and place of birth, nationality, address in country of origin, address in Brazil, amount of funds available to support ourselves, and a rough itinerary of our planned travel. A visa was stamped into our Canadian passports for ninety days, renewable for a fee at any federal government office. We were warned to apply for the extension, if needed, well in advance. It might not be granted if the old visa date had expired. Incidentally, Brazil requires most nationalities to obtain a visa *before* entering; if you enter without one, you're given seventy-two hours to leave. (Paul had obtained his visa in the Cape Verdes.)

We spent over one and a half days completing all of these formalities. Penny and Peter, of course, could not be left on the boat by themselves, so the hot, humid, harrowing days of dealing with officialdom also included them. But children are a real asset when dealing with officials, and they always seemed to break the ice for us. In South America, where boys are universally admired, Peter was so doted on by various officials that they sometimes hardly looked at our papers. Luckily Penny's self-image is strong, and she took it all in her stride. (And she was just as pleased as we were when Peter's three swimming lessons a day at the Natal Yacht Club left him able to swim the length of the pool. Four swimmers in the family!)

Clearing into a country, however, is not the end of it. Many countries, including Brazil, require yachts to obtain clearance out from *each* major port visited and *in* to the next large harbour, though smaller anchorages along the way might not necessitate a visit to the port authority. When we were ready to leave Brazil for French Guiana, we went through it all again, more or less in reverse order, before finally reporting to the harbour officials for our summary clearance papers. The clearance is usually considered good for twenty-four hours before you depart the harbour area, so we usually start the departure paperwork on the morning before we are due to leave, and get a good night's sleep to recover from our running around before setting off on another passage.

In many harbours of the world, the officials dealing with yachts do not have a boat available to motor out to you. They may require you to tie up to a dock where they can board, do the paperwork, and also inspect the vessel and her contents. At other harbours, you may be requested to transport the officials in your own dinghy to the boat for inspection.

We have found officials, almost universally, to be honest. But in a couple of places we were asked for a bottle of liquor. This is usually in a poor country where there is a large import duty on things like Scotch whisky. The official might announce with regret that you have too many bottles on board to be allowed in without bonding or the payment of duty – yet if you were to give one bottle away the number would be sufficiently decreased to allow the rest to be cleared without any trouble.

Before officials come on board, we instruct Penny and Peter not to answer general questions, explaining that I will do all the answering. In all innocence they might correct something I have said, or perhaps talk about something on another boat that we would not wish discussed with officials. We don't have anything to hide, but as nothing invites distrust and suspicion more than contradictory answers to a question, we simply take the precaution of telling our voluble children how to behave.

Once the paperwork has been finished, we can all relax, and over a cup of coffee we'll ask the officials about cultural events and points of interest in the area. They are usually proud of their country and glad to pass on information.

Brazil was also the first country where theft was a major problem in two of the main harbours we visited (Natal and

Fortaleza), though not in the smaller ports. Both Natal and Fortaleza are well frequented by yachts, which anchor off the yacht club in an area where there are many local craft moving about. Both cities have an active and interesting night life to lure yachties away from their vessels at night: yet this is also an area hit by drought, and many people are extremely poor and to them such portable boat items as radios, tape recorders, compass, represent a great temptation.

We had no problems with theft, as we were always on board at night, usually getting back to the boat with Penny and Peter well before dark, eschewing the night life and the glitter. Because they knew we would be on board at night, other boats often anchored near us. We did not usually undertake a specific watch, but yachties are generally happy to keep a lookout for each other.

In Natal I foiled what I am sure was a robbery attempt on a French yacht anchored just upstream from us. I was sitting in the dark in our cockpit when I just happened to see a rowboat with three men in it approaching Serge's boat, which I knew had no one on board for the evening. I was suspicious because the boat was slowly approaching from the side not facing the shore. When one man made to climb on board, I took our spotlight and shone it directly on the men, who hastily pushed off and rowed away.

We first met Jean-Jacques Teyssèdre, his wife and two daughters on their 40-foot *Carpe Diem 3* in the Cape Verde Islands. They also sailed to Brazil, arriving in Fortaleza about six weeks after we had left. When we next saw them in French Guiana, Jean told us the following story.

Robberies had increased to such a level in Fortaleza that the foreign yachts were rafting together and taking turns standing watch through the night, as would-be thieves had started coming on board while people were asleep.

"One day an American yacht entered, but she did not want to raft up with us," said Teyssèdre. "In the small hours of the morning, as I stood watch in the cockpit, I heard a commotion and saw the man and his wife leap into their dinghy – to my astonishment the man was brandishing and firing a gun."

It seems that while the dauntless skipper and his wife slept, two robbers had boarded their boat. The owner woke with a start to see a hand reaching over him to take a pair of binoculars from a shelf above his berth. His bellow of alarm woke his wife and frightened the two boarders, who raced out of the cabin and jumped into their rowboat, making for shore.

The yacht's dinghy with outboard was alongside and, pausing only to check that his radio, sextant, and other valuables were missing, the American grabbed his pistol, then he and his wife jumped into their dinghy. He fired his gun at the robbers several times as the dinghy closed the distance. They were so close that the robbers abandoned their boat on the beach and ran for it, leaving their loot behind.

The incident was reported to the authorities, who claimed that they were virtually powerless to stop the thefts on yachts. They assured the yachtsman he had done the right thing by firing at the intruders, and that even if he had hit the robbers he would not have encountered any difficulties with the authorities. . . .

Pickpockets are also prevalent, especially in larger cities in Central and South America. I was pickpocketed successfully once, but then foiled two similar attempts later.

Here's the scoop, so to speak. I was standing in the aisle of a crowded city bus, working my way towards the door to get off. A young man in front of me "dropped" a handful of small change from his pocket, which spilt on the floor of the bus just as it was stopping. I bumped into him as he bent over to retrieve his change – and the line of people behind me accidentally bumped into me.

The man immediately behind me apologized as his briefcase hit my pocket. Then he pushed past, as if in a hurry. He certainly was in a hurry – the briefcase pushed against me had taken my attention as he lifted my wallet! In the few moments it took me to realize what had happened, both the man looking for his change and the actual thief had disappeared from view.

The next time someone "dropped" their change in front of me, however, I was ready, and I swung my hand down to protect my new wallet. It was already halfway out of my pocket into someone's hand and was knocked to the floor, where I retrieved it, happier to chase my wallet than the departing would-be thief. By the third attempt, I was quick enough to knock away the briefcase before the hand got to my wallet. Practice makes for fast reactions!

THE LURE
OF THE JUNGLE

18

As well as the problems on land in Brazil, we encountered difficulties in sailing the 1,200 miles along Brazil's northern coast. We did it in four hops of a few hundred miles each, stopping at the small river harbours of Areia Branca and Luis Correira, as well as at the large port of Fortaleza and anchoring off Salinopolis.

I hated these passages of two or three days, as the light, fickle winds all along the coast kept us rolling and slopping about, and the motion made me continuously seasick. We paralleled the coast, but we had to keep at least twenty miles offshore, as numerous sandbanks run out this far from land. Sick or not, we had to maintain a sharp lookout.

The main current along the coast was helpful, as it moved westward in the direction we were headed, but our friends Marius and Marie-Jeanne d'Alessandri on the French-registered cutter *Aura* warned us about a strong east-going counter-current near shore. They had sailed along this coast a few months earlier, but with two days of squalls and overcast skies were not sure of where they were. They hailed a fishing boat to ask for an exact position – and then sailed on. At dawn the next day they had still not had a fix, and, seeing the same fishing boat, came alongside to ask where they were for a second time.

"You are in exactly the same position as yesterday,"

Difficult passages . . . counter-current . . . strange anchorage . . .
the mighty Amazon . . . Belém . . . Manaus jungle experience . . .
piranha fish . . . lily-pad experiment . . . hammocks . . . alligator eyes
. . . luxury catamaran . . . never get married . . . sailing again

---

said the captain. "We haven't moved – and neither have you!"

Aura's log showed that the boat had travelled seventy miles – but during the night the counter-current had been moving the boat backwards at the same speed!

Our worst experience along this coast was at Salinopolis, where we arrived at our fourth Brazilian river port just at dusk. The darkness made it too dangerous to negotiate the sandbanks in front of the river harbour. But we could not go on, either, as we were now only a few miles from the Amazon Basin, and it would have been suicidal to try to pick our way through the islands, shoals, and debris of that legendary body of water in the dark.

It was with great trepidation that we anchored a couple of miles offshore *in the open sea*. There was little chance of sleep as *Lorcha* noisily rose and fell with every passing wave in our twenty-foot-deep anchorage and the internal cables rattled endlessly in our hollow mast as the boat rolled from side to side all through the night.

We were only too thankful to be on our way at first light, and soon we were entering the turbulent waters of the Amazon outflow. Although we knew that the Rio Pará, the Amazon tributary that would take us to Belém, was fifty miles wide at its mouth, it was a very strange experience to be headed up a river with water stretching as far as eye could see on either side and an amazing array of small islands ahead. We could still have been on the open ocean, and only our charts showed us we were going up a river, with the thick muddy waters, swirling with foam, logs, and other debris, confirming that we were in the vicinity of land.

The Amazon is not to be approached without some planning. It is the second-longest river in the world at 3,191 miles. The mouth was discovered in 1500 by Vicente Yáñez Pinzón, who named it the Mar Dulce or Fresh-Water Sea – and no wonder, for the various tributaries comprising the river delta stretch over an incredible two hundred miles. The river system is responsible for twenty-five per cent of the world's fresh-water supply, and the vegetation provides the world with forty per cent of its oxygen, so the conservation or exploitation of this largely unexplored region will have interesting international repercussions.

And do the famous female Amazon warriors really exist? In history they do – it was the battles fought by the Spanish explorer Francisco de Orellana during his west-east descent of the river in 1541–2 that gave rise to the legends of the world's fiercest female tribal warriors living here. But Don Starkell, whose book *Paddle to the Amazon* records the challenging 12,000-mile canoe journey made by him and his son Dana all the way from Winnipeg to join the Amazon at Manaus and on to Belém, never encountered any Amazons, although he named his canoe *Orellana*.

The Starkells, paddling downstream with the current, sometimes made sixty miles a day. But with sail *and* motor we took three full days to battle the eighty-five miles up the Rio Pará against the full force of the current, which could reach ten knots. It was the wet season, which meant that the river was so full that we only dared to travel upriver during the four daylight hours of incoming tide. We anxiously planned each passage with our river charts to make sure we could find an anchorage at the side of the river or in the lee of an island at the end of this period. On our way upstream we constantly had to dodge whole trees and great masses of floating debris, and when we were at anchor and the tide turned, *Lorcha* jumped about like a wild thing, and we watched the anchor carefully in case it dragged. Looking at the waters rushing by our anchored vessel, Penny and Peter were

144

convinced *Lorcha* was still moving through the water. No wonder only about twelve yachts a year attempt this journey.

But it was more than worth the effort, for Belém – the "Bethlehem" that was the Starkells' goal for two long years – is a colourful and fascinating city. Its lively ten-block waterfront market entertained us for days, and there are many attractions to visit, including a first-class museum full of interesting artifacts and alive with the colourful history of the area. And then there is the pottery. Oh, for a boat big enough to load the ornate drinking-urns, the traditional plates and bowls, and the intricately carved and painted burial urns. They are simply wonderful.

Added to all this was the fact that the Iate (yacht in Portuguese) Clube de Pará was the largest and most luxurious yacht club we had ever stayed at. It has three restaurants and two swimming-pools, as well as saunas and showers, a dance hall, and a weekend orchestra. But what was more interesting to us was the fact that there was first-class security. We wanted to see more of the Amazon and we realized that the boat could be left at the club in perfect safety.

To many people, crossing the world's oceans on a yacht might seem like the ultimate experience – but Penny and Peter were more excited about the 1,000-mile aeroplane trip we would be taking westward to Manaus, the capital of the Amazonas State. We hoped to spend a day in the jungle before taking five days to travel the 952 miles down the river back to Belém on a catamaran cruise ship. Even though we would be on another boat, it would still be a break from doing our own navigating, nightwatches, provisioning, and cooking.

Wanting to explore the jungle wasn't as unusual as we thought, because on our first day in Manaus we met a local free-lance guide, Antonio Perez, who took visitors on just such trips.

"I could take you for only a day trip," said Antonio. "But it's much better to go for two or three days. If you want to see birds and animals, we must go at least sixty miles out of Manaus, and that means travelling by river and road. We'll be sleeping overnight in hammocks."

"We're in your hands, Antonio," we said.

At six o'clock the next morning we were on the ferry to Careiro on the south bank, followed by an hour's trip on an overcrowded bus along a bumpy section of the Trans-Amazon Highway to the Araca River, where we transferred to a motorized canoe. The jungle sped past us on both riverbanks and it took another hour to reach an isolated three-room clapboard house on stilts, under which cows, pigs, and chickens were sheltering from a sudden tropical downpour which had caught us midstream.

We were in the jungle.

The Amazon region is the land of the Caboclos, of mixed Amazon Indian and Portuguese blood. To encourage settlement, the government gives any family with a few cows, pigs, chickens, and ducks twenty hectares of land if they settle here for a prescribed number of years. The settlers we saw tend their herds and raise some vegetables, but mostly they hunt and fish and generally live off the land. Meanwhile, the original primitive Amazon Indians have been pushed back to reservations where tourists are forbidden to visit without special government permission.

Antonio was a Caboclo, and the house he took us to was typical of those we saw along the riverbanks. Our room, up six steep wooden steps, was bare except for a table, a bench, two stools, some old Christmas decorations, four hammocks – and a freshly caught armadillo in the old kerosene fridge.

The efficient Antonio, fluent in four languages, had brought all the necessary supplies with him and he soon cooked a magnificent lunch in record time as we rested. He was helped by the two young brothers, Manuel and Estevan Santos Lima, who owned the house and were presumably used to Antonio's turning up with wide-eyed visitors.

Another brother soon arrived, paddling his dugout canoe, the basic mode of transportation in this area, and we wandered down to the water's edge to see several still-alive piranha fish, a surprisingly good eating fish when fried.

Antonio was eager to show us his Amazon, and we soon piled into a canoe and headed upriver. Kingfishers, egrets, marsh hens,

146

vultures, and hawks lined the banks, as well as many other species of birds we didn't recognize. The colossal cow-faced manatee (sea cow) raised its snout from time to time. Then Peter saw a pink dolphin jump.

I was doubtful. *Pink?* But our guide quickly pointed out another, and then a few more.

It was the Boto, the pink Amazon river dolphin, one of the few fresh-water species. And he *is* dusky pink! We saw them showing their flanks as well as their backs as they rolled on the surface of the shallow water, and they were not small either, as they reach up to 10 feet in length. They were plentiful, but seemed more timid than their seagoing cousins. We never saw one closer than sixty feet.

The Boto is regarded as having mysterious powers, and our guide told us that, according to local legend, it has the magical power to turn itself into a good-looking young man. He might go to any party held in a village along the riverbank and seduce a young woman with his diabolical charm.

In the more remote parts of the Amazon, when a girl becomes pregnant and the father-to-be is not identified, the blame is placed on the mysterious Boto, who was able to bewitch the girl and take his pleasure. No more strange, I suppose, than many of the other legends and tales involving these wonderful mammals about whose life cycles and habits we know so little.

We saw many fishermen along the banks in their dugout canoes, and paused to watch a man standing in his vessel, bow drawn and arrow about to fly. Many of the 1,800 identified species of fish in the Amazon are fruit-eaters. Fishermen wait silently under berry-laden branches overhanging the water. The fruit falls, the fish surfaces, and the arrow strikes.

It was the first time during our entire year of travel that Penny and Peter were left almost speechless, so struck were they by the wonders of the completely new world they had entered.

"Okay," said Antonio. "Let's test the lily-pads."

The Brazilian lily-pad (Victoria Regis) is the symbol for the region. The flower blooms white, turns pink within forty-eight hours, and dies rapidly. A new saucer-shaped leaf, or lily-pad, forms overnight. Its huge distinctive leaf, sometimes reaching a diameter of two metres, is said to be strong enough to hold a five-year-old.

Peter was more excited than anyone about testing the theory. It was a real experiment and only he, as the resident five-year-old, could do it! Antonio had to positively restrain him from leaping out of the canoe and onto the pad. Peter's little rump went through the first leaf, but not so fast that we couldn't see that, lying flat, the pad might hold him. We paddled over to another new-looking leaf and I gently lowered him onto the sparkling pad . . .

It held!

"You know, I've never seen that done before," said Antonio.

"In fact," he continued, "I've never taken children into the jungle before. I'm amazed at how well they've adapted. They're better than some of the grown-ups I've had!"

With Estevan paddling from the bow and Antonio steering from the stern, the canoe slid silently from the river-lake of Mamore up the Violoa Creek. Within a minute of turning off the main branch of the river, we were in dense jungle. Branches tore at our shoulders, vines and boughs brushed our faces, and all hands were busy keeping the various growths from lashing back at us. Soon the vegetation was so thick that the air darkened. We had to look up to see light.

Penny and Peter were bug-eyed.

The water was black and still, perfectly mirroring the growth, until we had the illusion that an impenetrable wall confronted us. As the canoe meandered through the thick growth in the shallow water, we were so totally disoriented that we could have never have found our way back without a guide.

Parrots squawked at us from the trees, a large river snake wriggled past, and monkeys chattered in the distance, occasionally visible as they leapt from treetop to treetop. Enormous colourful butterflies – many a bright turquoise – flitted about, enthralling the children with their variety and size.

The time passed quickly and we got back to the house just as dusk was falling. There were surprisingly few mosquitoes inside, but we pulled the wooden shutters to keep out the bats. A short nap in the hammocks was called for and we swung them down from the walls.

"Are you sure I won't fall out in the middle of the night?" asked Peter, valiantly trying to master the technique of getting in.

We were all tired after our long and unusual day and we lay thankfully on the hammocks, swinging gently as we listened to the hiss of the gas lantern and the night sounds of the jungle.

"Come with me, Penny and Peter," said Antonio, as soon as it was dark. "You can see some red, shining alligator eyes right from the back step."

"You mean they're that close?" asked Peter a little apprehensively.

Antonio shone a powerful torch at the water's edge about twenty metres from the house and we were able to pick out the bright-red glow from the eyes of at least three small alligators. The children held on tightly to the back railing as they drank in the scene.

But our holiday was not yet over, for the next afternoon we were in Manaus, boarding the 500-ton, 170-foot catamaran *Pará*, the vessel that has been taking passengers Amazon-sightseeing since 1982. She has a capacity of 135 passengers, is fully air-conditioned, and has her own swimming-pool.

This voyage was a delight for all of us. Though we were still all living together in one tiny cabin with four bunks, we had all the space and amenities of the whole catamaran to enjoy, and we were never in the slightest worried about letting Penny and Peter have the run of the ship. This feeling of security increased when we found that they were the only children on board and had soon acquired a whole host of new aunts, uncles, and grandmothers. For though the children don't suffer from pangs of loneliness on board *Lorcha*, they open like flowers to the slightest interest from new adults.

All Paul and I had to do was eat our fill of tasteful buffet-style food, watch the shore go by, and enjoy the four land excursions included on the five-day passage. At times the river was so wide, we couldn't see either bank, and it was almost like being at sea. At other times we were close enough to the banks that we could wave to the people on the isolated huts on shore – or they would paddle out to the boat hoping the passengers would throw over goodies in plastic bags filled with air. And, indeed, at one narrow stretch of the river, about five hundred such bags were dropped over the side during an eight-hour period.

But the incident we enjoyed the most was meeting a cigar-smoking, rum-drinking old lady who as a teenager had helped lay the foundation stone of a more-than-a-century-old church.

A century-old church? That's right. For Maria de Purifacio was 128 years old.

Maria was swinging lazily on a hammock in her two-room house in Alter-do-Chao on the Tapajós River, where we had stopped for a shore excursion to the sandy beach that lay before the village.

A score of children, shyly offering us bead necklaces, led us to her house. A mixture of my broken Portuguese and some help from a Portuguese-speaking passenger-guide told us the secret of her longevity.

"Never get married. Your husband will only get jealous and cause you trouble and stress – which will shorten your life."

She drank the local rum and smoked cigars whenever she could get them and had had eight children by seven different men. Only one child, a women in her late eighties, was still living.

Her long, snowy-white hair was rolled up on the back of her head, and though she had lost all her teeth, she walked along with the aid of a cane and certainly had all her senses. She said she ate everything, but her diet was mostly fish and fruit. She had slept in a hammock all her life.

The jungle does not give up her secrets lightly and you won't discover the heart of the Amazon on this kind of trip. But it's an enjoyable way to see at least something of the waters and impenetrable banks of the world's second-largest river. We found that the time spent with other people had been good for all of us, and it was with renewed vigour and energy that we once more boarded our favourite little yacht.

We were ready to face the voyage down the mighty currents of the Rio Pará again and our next ocean passage, a distance of about four hundred miles to French Guiana.

Truth to tell, we could hardly wait to get sailing again.

COOKING
AT SEA

19

We were much more relaxed about our journey down the Rio Pará than we had been fighting our way upriver from the delta, and we upped anchor from our snug berth at the Belém Yacht Club at 1800 hours to begin our six-day passage to Cayenne, the capital of French Guiana.

In between our Amazon adventures in the interior, Paul had redesigned some of the interior of the boat, taking out our fore-and-aft table and settee, and replacing them with two athwartships benches and a dinette table, around which the four of us could sit more comfortably. The new arrangement also gave Penny and Peter a more useful working area, as they could now each spread their schoolwork or other projects along their own side of the table.

As we sped down the Rio Pará on the ebb tide, the children found their own creative use for our new table. They draped sheets over the top, put pillows in the new space underneath the table between the dinette benches, and snuggled down for a morning's reading, too involved with their new-found boat-house to come on deck for a last look at the bustling Ver-O-Peso waterfront market slipping slowly past on our starboard side.

It would be a somewhat strange passage downriver, as we would be stopping to anchor every few hours when the tide turned, and would have to find something to do during the hours of waiting for the tide to ebb

*New dinette . . . stocking up . . . banana cake . . . pressure cooker
. . . canned foods . . . sourdough . . . various breads . . . delta exit
. . . crossing the equator again . . . strong currents . . . leadline . . .
omelette pan . . . eggs . . . powdered milk . . . boat treats . . .
Cayenne*

---

again. With the dinghy securely lashed to the coach roof, we would not be going ashore – and who would have wanted to row through that current anyway? We would while away our at-anchor hours reading, doing schoolwork, and indulging in one of our favourite preoccupations on the water: cooking. Meals assume an overwhelming importance when one is far from land, and eating varied and appetizing food is a highlight of the day.

Our timing for lunch was perfect, as it was just on noon when we anchored off the island of Mosquiero, where we ate a simple cockpit lunch of boiled eggs on fresh wholemeal bread with carrot salad, finishing up with large, yellowy pieces of papaya so ripe that the rich juice ran down Peter's face to dribble between the teak cockpit slats.

Belém had been a surprisingly good stocking-up port and we had enough good fruit and vegetables to last us for at least two weeks, well beyond what we would need for our six-day passage.

Many people ashore seem to think we must have to live on dried beans and rice when voyaging, but this is just not so. While zucchinis, pineapples, carrots, and red tomatoes may only keep fresh for four to six days, we could always rely on eggplant, cucumbers, and green tomatoes to see us well through our second week at sea. We found that green cabbages keep fresh for at least four weeks, and we buy onions and potatoes in 10- and 20-kilo quantities, as these staples will last for two to three months. We had spent the previous morning at the Ver-O-Peso market, going from stall to stall to ensure that we bought the freshest possible produce. In my purchases I had included a bunch of yellow and a bunch of green bananas, and as soon as Peter had washed the papaya juice from his chin, I suggested to the kids that we might make a banana cake. They were happy to help.

We don't have an oven on *Lorcha* and I bake all our breads and cakes in a pressure cooker. This is partly because of lack of space, but also partly by choice, since oven cooking uses a lot of gas and heats the boat up very quickly. The kids and I would certainly not have been making a banana cake that sultry afternoon – the whole Amazon area being very close to the equator – if we had had to turn on an oven. It took Penny and me only about ten minutes to mix up the eggs, margarine, flour, and sugar, while Peter mashed up three ripe bananas. We spooned the mixture into a round baking tin and covered it with greaseproof paper, popping the whole thing into an inch and a half of water in the pressure cooker, where it would cook in about forty minutes.

We spent the rest of the afternoon lazily reading on deck before the kids set the table in the cockpit for an early dinner of avocados, followed by fish stew with eggplant, tomatoes, carrots, and potatoes. We upped anchor at 1800 hours to catch the evening ebb tide to our next anchorage, 33 kilometres (20 miles) downriver just south of the Colores light. We were all munching large pieces of freshly baked banana bread as we sat in the cockpit watching the distant, well-spaced shore lights spinning by. At 2200 hours we were safely anchored and ready for bed.

Next morning we were on the move again at 0730 hours. With the sail up, the motor running, and the tide pushing us along, we were making at least nine knots over the ground, and Penny scarcely had time to complete a day's schoolwork before we saw a mile of fish traps on the horizon, a sign that we were approaching our anchorage on the sandbanks just north of the headland of Ponta Taipu.

Lunch was a tomato salad, fresh pineapple, and a tin of the most delicious Brazilian vegetable paste on bread. One of the delights of travelling in different countries is that we get to try all sorts of new foods. Everyone knows that each country has its own special fruit and vegetables, but I had discovered quite different *canned* foods in each country too, though it was often quite some trick to decipher the label. I like to have a good selection of tins on board, as eating tinned food can be restrictive enough, without having to eat the same tinned food all the time. So I always make a point of buying and trying new tins when I can – and of buying tins in quantity when I find a food I like. I've never yet bought too much of something we all liked, though the converse was often true!

As well as the sensational vegetable paste (I had twelve cans stashed in the food-locker), I had made another discovery in Belém – sourdough culture. Imagine finding six small bottles of sourdough culture in a supermarket up the Amazon! Sourdough was used by cooks long before yeast was discovered, and early pioneers only knew of it as a mysterious self-replenishing substance that gave them sure-fire morning hotbread day after day. Knowing the way I anxiously overstock on my yeast supplies (terrified that I might run out on some remote island and be unable to bake bread), I can understand the way those early pioneers like the miners in the Klondike gold rush – who became known as "sourdoughs" – are reputed to have jealously guarded their sourdough starter, often carrying the floured dough in a pouch next to their skin to keep it safe.

I had already processed my precious culture into a bubbling starter, so that afternoon Penny and I (Peter was busy with adding his new Brazilian stamps to his stamp collection) stirred up the pancake mixture, starting early as the dough has to stand for a couple of hours before it is ready for the final ingredients to be added.

We initially had planned on heading out of the Rio Pará to the open sea on the evening tide, but a spectacular squall with forty-knot winds came through at about 1700 hours, completely blotting out the nearby shoreline. It only lasted an hour, but as the sky was still very threatening, we decided to remain where we were overnight and leave on the morning tide.

Of course everyone was involved in making the pancakes for

supper. The sourdough recipe was delicious, and I was glad to be able to add something new to our flour-based lunch choices, courtesy of the trusty pressure cooker. We now had yeast bread, white or wholemeal, which took about three hours to mix, rise, and bake; cornbread, which took about an hour to prepare and cook; pan-fried milk-and-egg bread, which I could make in fifteen minutes and which was a good emergency standby; and now the pancakes, which could be mixed up the previous evening and left to stand overnight ready for cooking in the morning.

We were glad we had decided to anchor overnight, because the previous night's squall had washed the sky clear and the next morning was calm and sunny, with a pleasant breeze blowing. By 0630 hours the tide was slack and we were off, anxious to be as clear of the delta as possible before the tide turned again. Dolphins played at our bow, fish jumped at the stern, and a variety of brilliantly coloured butterflies and moths fluttered about us as they tried to land on the warm deck to sun themselves, where they made a bright pattern.

The delta is well buoyed for ocean freighters, and when we spotted an outgoing freighter well to port, we crossed over from our sandbank to follow her down the main channel. We celebrated our good run downriver with a present of modelling-clay for the kids, and while they squished and squashed their new toy, I did the same for the day's bread, which I left out on the coach roof to rise. Bread always seems to take so long to make, but it really takes only about ten minutes to mix up; the rest of the time is spent in waiting for it to rise, punching it down, and then waiting for it to rise again. (If I'm in a real hurry, I cook it after the first rising.) Today's lunch bread would be fresh and hot.

There was no trouble sailing through the muddy and still-turbulent waters of the delta and we were soon far from shore, out of the tidal ebbs and flows, with the water becoming bluer with every mile. We passed another landmark in our journey when we crossed the equator, back into the North Atlantic, in the afternoon. Everyone was anxious to see what new star patterns,

156

if any, we would see in the Northern Hemisphere that evening, but we were disappointed. The bright five-star Southern Cross was still clearly visible, though low in the sky, but we were still not able to see Polaris, the pole-star, which we now hadn't sighted for five months. I know the kids will be looking for it on every night of this passage. It was a lovely evening, and before going to bed, the children sang all the songs they knew, snuggling against Paul and me in the cockpit and watching the bright rising moon.

I was tired and irritable next morning after our first night of three-hour watches and was glad when the children got out their modelling-clay. At 0900 hours Paul was up and ready to do some sextant sights. Penny helps by writing down the index error, the time, and the angles, which she does neatly and well – more neatly than her schoolwork, in fact. Paul did another sight at noon and started muttering to himself when his sextant position showed a difference of about fifty miles between our position fix and the dead-reckoning position. We knew there was a strong ocean current along the coast, but that strong?

Even though we were one hundred miles offshore, our sextant position had us over relatively shallow water and Paul got out the leadline (a simple lead and line to measure depth) to see if it would touch bottom when he threw it over the side. Unfortunately just as he was swinging the lead, the line broke – and part of the line and the lead disappeared with a splash to sink we knew not how many feet! Paul wasn't too happy, but Penny and Peter thought it was great stuff, especially as they helped fashion a new leadline. Peter helped drill a hole in a new lump of lead (we carry spares of *everything*) and threaded wire through the hole he had made, while Penny assisted with the knots marking the depths on the line. Both were full of advice for Paul on how to do everything, and by the time the job was finished in the late afternoon, we had cleared the suspected shallow patch of water. So we still weren't sure of our exact position.

A quick and easy supper was called for, so I made nice fat

Spanish omelettes, filled with onions, tomatoes, and potatoes. We carry a special omelette and crepe pan on board, because Paul makes great crepes and the pan really makes omelette-cooking a pleasure for me, as the eggs never stick. I had visited my favourite fresh-egg stall in Belém before we left and bought four dozen unrefrigerated eggs (they stay fresh longer) to take with us. On very long passages, or when we're headed for some remote island where I don't think there'll be much in the way of stores, I'll stock up with twelve dozen or more eggs. They keep fresh for eight to ten weeks if I turn them over every couple of days.

I was up at seven the next morning after a lousy night with the boat pitching and tossing because there was no wind. I was feeling tired and irritable, so it was not a morning to sit down and do schoolwork with Penny. We had cereal for breakfast with powdered milk, and as we had finished the box, I gave it to the children, as I knew the cut-out puppets on the back would keep them occupied for a couple of hours.

If anyone had told me before I started voyaging that I would quickly become used to margarine instead of butter (too expensive) or powdered milk instead of fresh milk (not available), I would have thought them daft, but we soon passed from toleration to acceptance, if not enjoyment. What I did find out, though, was that there is a wide range in the quality of powdered milk. When I'm faced with unfamiliar brands, I buy small quantities of each so that I can do a taste test on them. For if we buy a brand that won't mix and doesn't taste good, no one will drink it. But a good-tasting brand which mixes well can taste just like the real thing. Well, almost.

After a lunch of grilled-cheese sandwiches and an avocado salad, we all had a fresh-water shower while Paul worked out the day's sunsights. They confirmed that we were making forty miles a day with the current, so it was time to be sewing a French courtesy flag; if the current kept up, we would be arriving in Cayenne the next day.

Paul cooked an early supper of corned-beef hash, and as we

158

were going so well, I felt it was time to treat us all to a bar of chocolate. The psychology of treats while voyaging is all-important, and just the right balance needs careful planning. They can lift our spirits after a dispirited day's sailing, or mark a celebration such as the mid-point of a voyage – or any other occasion you can think of, such as the fast passage we were now making.

On *Lorcha*, treats include chocolate bars, sweet biscuits, jars of olives, dried fruit, canned nuts, and special cake mixes. We don't have them often – that's why they're called treats – and I'm glad that Penny and Peter can still ooh and aah when we open a packet of chocolate cookies and that they can still say *"Thank you, Mama"* as they slowly savour each bite. I make sure, however, to stock up on treat items when I see them, as there may be a few months in poorer countries when I can't buy such things as chocolate. On *Lorcha*, we drink plain water ninety per cent of the time, so a shore treat will be a glass of cordial or lemonade – though we'll all opt for cold milk if it's available.

The weather must have responded to our on-board celebrations as *Lorcha* soared through the night on a reach in 15 to 20 knots of wind. I woke up at 0700 hours feeling rested and cheerful. My body has usually adjusted to broken sleep patterns on the third night out (our fifth from Belém), and the steady wind, with no sail banging, had also helped.

"Land ho!" called Paul, spotting the off-lying islands of French Guiana, and by lunch-time Penny was sewing the last seam on our French flag while the rest of us were figuring out the channel and entrance to Cayenne. There were rocks, islands, and light-buoys to find, and Peter was busy trying to be the first to sight a buoy and read off its number. We had timed our arrival perfectly, as Cayenne lies at the mouth of the Cayenne River and it's best to negotiate the off-lying shoals on a rising tide, which we were doing.

After being the solitary yacht in Belém when we left, we could now see at least forty boats at anchor in Cayenne. And from the small figures waving as we got closer, there were also many vessels with children aboard. That was good news, because Penny would be celebrating her eighth birthday here, and as with such celebrations ashore, a party would be in order.

THE TURTLES OF
FRENCH GUIANA

20

The bustling scene of all those yachts at anchor and the to-ing and fro-ing of many dinghies in the harbour of Cayenne was creating a very different scene from when Christopher Columbus sailed along the coast in 1498; at that time he pronounced it not only barren but scantily populated and seemingly uninhabitable.

The French took possession of the territory in 1626, and it passed through both English and Dutch hands until 1809, when it once again reverted to the French, who this time held on to it. By 1852 the whole country was devoted to the notorious French convict settlements, of which Devil's Island became the best-known. Although the last prisoners left in 1953 and have been replaced by tourists (but not in the same cells!), today the French are building complete Laotian villages on the mainland for modern refugees from that strife-torn region.

Cayenne is one of the traditional stopping-off points for French cruising boats, who by law can only take so much currency out of France. The result is that most French boats are working their cruises. Happily for them, there are many French colonies, like French Guiana, where they can stay for three months to a year and earn some money, enjoying their work-then-cruise lifestyle.

Cayenne harbour was rather like a small village. From six o'clock in the morning the anchorage was alive with

---

dinghies busily ferrying people to the onshore showers, dads to work – and sometimes mums too – and children to school. Unfortunately for Penny and Peter, however, the children were mostly on a day-long schedule, often returning to their boats around seven in the evening. They even went to school on Saturday mornings.

Of the fifty boats at anchor, forty-five were French, with the occupants of forty of those boats involved in some occupation or other; two were Swiss, one was Belgian, one was Australian, and us. Most of the men were involved in the building or electrical trades or worked in one of the sawmills, with women finding jobs as nurses and teachers. There seemed to be a big demand for English-teachers and we were told we could get work here if we wanted. Two travelling boat doctors would consult informally with patients on board, while one vessel was completely equipped with dental tools, including a reclining chair.

When there was no work available, two or three boat captains would get together and head for the interior, to pan for gold or collect tarantula spiders, which would evidently fetch up to $100 apiece in France. Of course, when these expeditions returned, they would never divulge whether they had found any gold or not – but we always reckoned they would probably make more money out of spiders.

But while panning for gold sounded romantic, the story that most interested us here was that of the giant Luth turtles who come every year between April and July to lay their eggs on the beach at Les Hattes, 200 kilometres away. We borrowed a car from one of the other boat people and organized a two-day trip to the beach, to allow us to spend the night on the sand to watch the turtles come ashore. Even though we would be leaving *Lorcha* in an open anchorage in swift-flowing current, she would be safe enough, as everyone in our marine village looked out for everyone else with real community spirit. There were no theft or robbery problems here.

There were very few roads in French Guiana; significantly, the word "Guiana" is the Amerindian word meaning "land surrounded by water", and water is everywhere. As well as its seacoast, French Guiana is criss-crossed with rivers and marshes, which combine with the dense rain forests to make the building of inland roads impossible. All interior travel is by river boat or aeroplane. The only road is the coast road from Cayenne to Les Hattes which loops up to St. Laurent, fifty miles or so up the Maroni River.

We arrived at Les Hattes at four o'clock in the afternoon and the kids lost no time in dashing onto the beach while we parked the car. Soon we heard excited shouts.

"Mama, Papa, come quick. There's a turtle on the beach."

She had just come out of the water and we stood well back as she dragged herself ashore; we knew that if the turtles are disturbed when they first come out of the sea, they will return to the water without laying their eggs. Slowly this 450-kilo (1,000 pound) grey-backed turtle came up the steep sand. When she came to a spot she seemed to like, she shuffled around, then scrunched down and started to hollow a space to settle in. Next it was the turn of her back flippers to start burrowing a hole, which she dug about twenty-eight inches deep. It was hard work and the digging took her about an hour.

There were now four or five people, tourists like ourselves, watching her, the only people on this three-mile strip of sandy beach. The turtle showed no sign of fear, but imperturbably went on throwing the sand up around her.

When both she and the "nest" are ready, a female turtle will drop anywhere from 40 to 150 eggs. It sounds a lot – but only one turtle will return to this beach from every 3,000 eggs laid. It will take fifteen years, but this one incredible animal will come back to within five hundred yards of her birthplace, perhaps having travelled as far as China in the meantime.

Though the giant Luth turtle is not yet an endangered species, there is concern for the future, and the Greenpeace Foundation has been working in French Guiana for two years to try to help expand the population. They have made some interesting discoveries.

"We used to collect the eggs by hand to incubate them," said Frédérique Rimblot of Greenpeace, showing us around the house that served as a turtle hatchery. "But we found that once human hands had touched the eggs, they didn't hatch."

Now they place a net bag in the nest just as the turtle starts dropping her soft-shelled eggs, and gather them this way. We watched later as Frédérique simply lifted the turtle's back flipper aside to catch the eggs as they dropped. The turtle did not even notice that some of her eggs were being taken.

After her eggs were safely laid, we watched our turtle go to work to fill up her hole with sand, which not only protects the eggs, but keeps them at the required incubation temperature.

The sand flew everywhere as her powerful front flippers threw the sand behind her. With the eggs covered and hidden, the turtle continued to throw sand in all directions around her nest, taking a few steps one way and a few steps another. She devoted as much care to hiding her eggs as she did to preparing the nest, and by the time she was finished, we couldn't see where the eggs were.

"Gosh," said Penny. "Where *are* the eggs? It looks as though a bulldozer's been here."

Only when she was completely satisfied – and thoroughly exhausted – did the turtle start to drag her huge body down to the water, never again to see her eggs, or her offspring. She would repeat the whole incredible performance four or five times during the season.

At dusk, the turtles really started coming ashore, and even though the mosquitoes were out and biting, we stood and watched another four or five of them laying their eggs. Some came right up the beach, leaving themselves with a long haul back to the water, while others stayed as close to the water's edge as they could, while still remaining above the high-water mark. Some looked at the sea as they worked; others faced the land.

Though about four or five cars drove up during the night, the beach was never crowded, with only a handful of people around at any one time to watch the scene. At one point it was deserted except for us.

Even the children never tired of watching the process, and soon Penny had found an old plastic bottle with which she could pour sea water over the heads of the tired turtles.

"Look at her, Mama," she said sympathetically. "She's lifting her head and looking straight at me. I think she's asking for more."

And off she dashed down the beach to fill her plastic jug.

During the night, we were also able to see another incredible sight, the baby turtles making their way out of the sand where eggs had been laid seventy days before, and scuttling down the beach to the water. When they popped their heads out, they made straight for the sea without hesitation or even a quick look around, almost as if they were aware that this was a danger period for them with dogs ready to eat, vultures ready to pounce, and careless tourist feet ready to squash.

The Greenpeace people made another discovery about the baby turtles. When they incubated the eggs ashore, they kept their baby turtles for forty-eight hours, carefully feeding them nutrients before taking them down to the water's edge. To their surprise, when their "stronger" turtles got into the ocean water they promptly drowned.

"Now we bury the two-day-old babies in twenty-eight inches of sand," said Marc Bretnacher of Greenpeace. "Like the other babies, these land-raised turtles have to form a turtle ladder over each other to get to the surface. They have to use their muscles in this way and then walk down the beach to prepare themselves for the buffeting of the sea."

The Greenpeace people also later realized that, in some

inexplicable way, the sand burial was also necessary to give the turtle the necessary homing instinct to one day return to the beach to lay her eggs.

From one hole we saw forty-eight babies emerge, one after the other, forming a marching line with little turtles four feet apart making their determined way into the sea – where they would face the hundred other dangers that would take the lives of so many of them.

It was almost midnight before I could get Penny and Peter into the car to get a few hours' sleep.

"But promise, *promise* you'll wake us within a *very* few hours – that is, if we *do* fall asleep – to see some more turtles," demanded Peter.

It was just about dawn when two French tourists came running along the almost deserted beach and knocked on the car door.

"Can you help?" they asked. "There's a turtle wedged in a tree and she can't get out."

Penny and Peter were first out and they scampered along the beach ahead of us. The French tourists led the way, along with Marc Bretnacher and Frédérique Rimblot from Greenpeace, who had also been called to help.

The turtle was indeed in trouble. She had laid her eggs nearby during the night and on returning to the sea had tried to force her way through the branches of a dead tree lying on the sand. Now she was well and truly trapped, with one badly cut flipper caught over a branch and her head badly cut. She could move neither forward nor back.

"We'll have to cut the branches in front of her with machetes," said Marc, swinging his blade high in the air.

Somehow the turtle understood we were there to help, and she remained motionless even though the chips of wood flew about her face. After the front branches came the hard part – chopping through the thick branch that held her flipper, and persuading her to turn around, since if she tried to go forward she would become even more entangled. The machetes chopped and six of us stood on her seaward side, ready to try to push her

450-kilogram body in the right direction. I knelt down beside her and kept up a running monologue.

"Mama Turtle, you've got to turn around. I know it's hard, but you have to go up the beach again until you're free from this goddamn tree."

The branch split, everyone pushed, and, though she hesitated, Mama Turtle started to turn around in her narrow prison. We cheered like anything as slowly, slowly, breathing deeply, her big body revolved, pushing heavily against the smaller branches until she was free.

But our troubles were not yet over. Exhausted though she obviously was – she puffed and gasped for breath in her distress – she now continued to try to make her laboured way *up* the beach and away from the sea. We knew she would die in the day's heat if she remained on the sand, and we ringed her once more to try to persuade her back towards the ocean.

"Here's some water," said Penny, pouring cooling sea water over the turtle's head as she rested for a few minutes.

Whenever she tried to move, we all pushed the exhausted and injured animal in the direction of the sea. It was a long, slow, agonizing procession – but at last we reached the shallows. Mama Turtle remained stationary in her natural surroundings and we stood back to let her take what comfort she could from the cold water. Then, to our utter astonishment, she started to head once more for the beach.

It seemed to be an instinctual move – but one we knew was also suicidal. Our hours of close connection with her had changed her from a dumb, helpless animal into a friend, a friend who now needed our help more than ever. Once more we stood on her shore side and, with a rope attached to the tail of her shell, worked her around until she was facing the sea again, using her natural buoyancy to get her into deeper water. We kept the pressure on till we were up to our thighs – and she was swimming.

With a nod of her head, which seemed to say she understood, she swam off, but strangely enough she still did not swim out to sea but skirted the beach for over a kilometre until, just opposite the village of Les Hattes, she looked towards her friends keeping pace with her along the shore and swooped underwater to head at last into the open ocean.

We were walking slowly back to the car when suddenly Peter gave a shout.

"Look, Mummy," he said in a panic. "That vulture's got a baby turtle in its mouth."

We ran towards the vulture, yelling and waving our arms, but in vain. He flew off with his catch. But Peter found another youngster in the spot where the vulture had been. The tiny creature was in a blind panic and was racing away from the direction of the sea.

"Help it. Help it," sobbed Peter.

We picked the baby up in a nest of sand and carried him down past the grass to where he could make his way more easily on the hard-packed sand. He used his tiny flippers to race along, with Peter shepherding him all the way. In time he plopped into the shallow water and we all watched as he started swimming – and soon the water was over his tiny head and we could only see ripples as he swam out to sea.

If Peter can continue to look after animals – and human beings – weaker than himself, all his life, we'll be very proud of our son. As it is, that picture of our five-year-old anxiously shepherding that tiny animal to safety is one I'll carry in my mind forever.

Back in Cayenne, Peter came to the rescue again – to our rescue! We had arrived with only $100 to our name, much too small a sum with which to be at large internationally and travelling with two small children. For one reason or another we could not use our credit cards for cash in Cayenne – and our normally efficient Canadian bank seemed unable to expedite the telexing of funds. It took thirty-one days for money to be forwarded to us from Canada, so our budget was down to $25 a week!

The person who contributed the most to our getting through this period was *Lorcha's* youngest crew member.

Cayenne is located just up the River Compte, and rivers usually mean fish. Peter at five years old was an avid, and by now experienced, fisherman. He knew all about our budget problems because suddenly there was no money for the treats the children like to enjoy ashore, especially after an ocean passage. No money for the occasional ice cream was serious business.

"Don't worry, Mama," said Peter, getting out his fishing-lines. "I can catch supper for us every night."

And to our surprise he proceeded to do just that. No matter that what he was catching was the lowly catfish. On every incoming tide, there was Peter using dough, which he mixed himself, bread, old cheese rind, or any bit of throwaway vegetable scrap, sitting at *Lorcha*'s stern and reeling 'em in.

In the end we grew tired of catfish.

"It's absolutely wonderful, Peter," I would say after the fifth straight day of catfish. "But I think we can afford omelettes tonight."

"Are you sure, Mama?" Peter would say anxiously. "I'm not tired, you know. I can easily get some more."

Honour was only satisfied when we arranged for Peter's fish catches to go to a cat on board another yacht every so often, but keeping *Lorcha* supplied for the balance of the week.

DEVIL'S ISLAND

21

We met Willi Gyger, a Swiss-born missionary, and his American wife and twelve-year-old daughter, both named Beatrice, the way we meet a lot of people – through the children. Penny was wheeling our small cart through the supermarket in Cayenne when she literally bumped into Beatrice the elder.

"Hello," said Beatrice in a friendly manner. "Where have you come from?"

As the Gygers have lived on and off in Cayenne for an astonishing thirty years, they pretty well know everybody there, so Beatrice realized Penny had to be a visitor.

"Oh, we're on a yacht," replied Penny. "Would you like to meet my mother?"

There are few North American visitors in Cayenne and before long we found ourselves having lunch with Willi and Beatrice. They were a friendly and fascinating couple and, of course, remembered the days when there were only a few thousand people in the "village" of Cayenne.

For a hundred years the whole of French Guiana, one-sixth the size of France, served as a vast and rambling penal colony. Between 1852 and 1952, thousands of desperate men, France's most-wanted criminals, were exiled to spend the rest of their lives there. It was not until 1946 that France started phasing out her now-notorious prison colony, with the last

Cayenne missionaries . . . penal colony . . . Îles du Salut . . . Papillon
. . . Autorité de Prison . . . mournful mourous . . . Devil's Island
. . . sharks . . . Henri Charrière's house . . . Dreyfus's bench

prisoners released from prison (but not French Guiana) in 1952, just a couple of years before the Gygers started their evangelical missionary work in Cayenne. They were the first people we met who actually knew many of those newly released prisoners. They met many old and destitute former detainees in those early days, and tried in various ways to help where they could.

"We hired one old man as the gardener," said Beatrice. "One of his jobs was also to keep an eye on the baby. He had been in prison and badly treated for so long that he couldn't believe we would trust him with our, at that time, only child, and he also never quite believed it when I would call out to him to have a cup of tea with us. It wasn't just the simple invitation that overwhelmed him, but the fact that I took the trouble to serve it in china cups and saucers. He hadn't seen those things for twenty years."

The Gygers were also a source of information about the Îles du Salut, the most famous section of the penal colony. For it was to these islands that the most hardened convicts – and also the political prisoners – were banished, with Devil's Island made famous by Henri Charrière in his book *Papillon*.

"We were there ten years ago," said Willi. "At that time there were few tourists and very little public information about the islands available. France had closed the penal colony and wanted to hide the whole thing under a blanket."

With the establishment in the 1970s of a space centre in Kourou on the mainland opposite, however, interest was again focused on the infamous islands, and this increased when a radar tracking station was built on Île Royale. The population of

Kourou exploded, and many foreigners visiting the space station also wanted to visit Les Îles du Salut. Cautiously, lines of communication were established. The eight-room Auberge, built from the old prison mess-hall as an accommodation centre for the rocket people, now began to take in other paying guests.

"Well, that sounds interesting," I said. "I think we'll make the islands our next stop–how would you like to come with us?"

A three-day holiday was all the time the Gygers could take off from their work, and armed with hammocks and blankets we set off on the ten-hour sail. It wasn't exactly the pleasant, exciting voyage we had planned for the Gygers, as the choppy waves made Willi incredibly seasick, and though we dragged a fishing-line all the way, the fresh-fish dinner I had envisaged turned into a what-shall-I-do-with-a-can-of-corned-beef supper.

But the Gygers were interesting company and the kind of thoughtful guests one appreciates on a small boat. Even though it was getting dark by the time we finished supper, they took their hammocks and blankets off the boat and went down the narrow pathway to find a spot among the falling-down prison buildings to spend the night.

The next day we decided to row over to Île St. Joseph, as it is one of the most interesting islands to walk around, with several old prison buildings still standing. We strolled along the recently cleared cobblestone pathways from one cell complex to another, picking fresh mangoes on the way.

The clear blue sea, with its white pounding surf, fringed with tall, swaying palm trees, was always in view – an ironic contrast to the pitiful conditions in which the convicts were forced to live. The solitary-confinement cells, half underground, with dirt floors, had no bunks, and the only light was from a six-inch (15 cm)-square grilled window ten feet (3 metres) above the floor. Other dark, dank cells had enough room for a man to lie full-length on the wooden board that served as a bunk, but there was barely enough width to stretch one's arms full-length.

We discovered a labyrinth of walls, exercise yards, and cell blocks dotted all over the island, a complex of buildings here, a single large block there. Many of the brick and stone buildings

174

were in quite good condition, with original numbers still on some cells and the odd painting on a stone wall still intact.

I saw Beatrice searching through bricks, turning them over and putting them aside, and asked what she was looking for.

"If you find a brick with A.P. stamped on it," she told me, "it shows that it's a brick made by the prisoners. They're a sort of collectors' item nowadays."

The A.P. stands for Autorité de Prison, and soon we were all looking for such bricks, finding one for the Gygers and one for us.

A small detachment of the French Foreign Legion occasionally camps on Île St. Joseph to clear the pathways and keep the worst of the jungle vines from the major prison complexes. We came across one unit hard at work, and were surprised to find the Legionnaires speaking mostly in English, Scottish, and Irish accents; we didn't stop to socialize.

We spent the next day walking around Île Royale, the largest island at roughly half a mile (900 metres) long; it was the former prison colony administrative centre and had the most developed housing, some prison blocks, a church, and a hospital. It is the island most developed for tourism today, with a daily ferry service from Kourou, and its Auberge is now able to accommodate up to fifty people and offers a splendid dining-room with a clear view over Devil's Island.

The hotel has an interesting way of keeping its fish fresh. When the fishermen catch the large 100-kilo mourous (grouper) which abound in these waters, they bring them to the island's jetty and "tether" them through the gills to a mooring buoy. It's not unusual to see four or five captured mourous swimming mournfully around as they wait for the call from the hotel dining-room.

It's less than a two-hour sail from Île Royale to the mainland port of Kourou and we dropped the Gygers off without incident the next day, returning to the islands to visit the last, and perhaps the most colourful, island in the group – Devil's Island.

"Look on this side, just beside us – two sharks," Paul said as we headed through the large ocean swells and the 2-knot current in the narrow channel between Île Royale and Devil's Island in the dinghy, the only way to reach the island.

"Don't call attention to them," I hissed, pointing to Peter and Penny. "And watch the swells."

"Where are the sharks?" demanded Penny, not one whit distracted.

There are fewer sharks these days, however, than there were fifty years ago. Most of the nearly seven thousand prisoners who passed through the penal system here were buried at sea. The body was laid in one of the island's only two coffins and loaded into a rowboat. As the boat put out to sea, the chapel bell would toll and in a few minutes the coffin would be held over the side of the boat so that the body could slide out of the open foot into the swirling seas. In time the sharks learned that the tolling of the bell was, for them, a dinner-bell, and the sound of it brought them swarming to the Baie des Cocotiers.

The increasing number of sharks did not, of course, upset the authorities one bit. They served as auxiliary guards to keep the hapless prisoners from even thinking of trying to escape.

But though few did manage to get away, one prisoner who did, and who told the story of Devil's Island to the world, was Henri Charrière. And as the surf carried us over the rocks to scramble ashore, we told the kids about him and set out to look for "Papillon's" house among the ruins still standing. Houses rather than prison blocks were the form of accommodation here, where only up to fifteen prisoners were ever left. They built their own houses, dug their own gardens, and fended for themselves without guards, sometimes left alone for months on end as weather conditions prevented any small vessel from landing on the surf-pounded rocky island.

Their diet would have been whatever they could grow – and coconuts, which grew in profusion. Growing wild now, the green fruit were perhaps one to two feet deep beneath our careful footsteps, with more and more young coconut trees trying to establish themselves wherever there was the minutest space.

It was eerie trying to hack our way through the luxuriant

undergrowth, but we also wanted to see if Captain Alfred Dreyfus's bench of stone was still in existence.

"Don't wander too far," I called to the kids, worried that if they got lost in the thick undergrowth we might have difficulty finding them again.

We hacked and picked our way through, discovering a sort of path blazoned with white marks on the trees, and quite suddenly we were on the east end of the island and able to make our way to the highest spot – not the sort of height you saw in the movie *Papillon*, where the reckless prisoner threw himself from a great height to escape his jail on a raft of coconuts, but enough that one could sit and watch the crashing, pounding surf below.

And it was indeed Captain Alfred Dreyfus's still-standing stone bench that we sat on as we recounted the story to Peter and Penny – the story of an innocent man, the victim of anti-Semitism, who served eight years of exile on Devil's Island on a false political treason charge until, amidst great uproar at home, he was deemed innocent in 1897 and freed, one of the few men sent to French Guiana who ever saw France again.

It was perhaps a sobering history lesson for Penny and Peter, but though they oohed and aahed as we recounted it, they were soon off and skipping back to the dinghy. For them it had been a great day of exploring, adventure, hacking out new trails with the machete, and enjoying fresh green coconut juice in the warm sun.

We had watched the same birds, cracked open coconuts from the same trees, sat on the same stone bench as those prisoners of long ago – but we thanked our lucky stars that we were free to up-anchor and continue our voyaging just when we wanted.

OCEAN
FISHING

22

I t was just past noon when I lifted the anchor from the bottom of the Baie des Cocotiers, Île Royale. Penny was below decks pushing the anchor chain aside in the chain box to make it run freely, and Fiona was on the helm. As we motored out of the bay, we waved goodbye to our friends on *Ev*, a French ketch with Philippe and Maggie and their two sons on board. We had first met them in the Canary Islands, caught up to them in the Cape Verdes, and again shared an anchorage with them in French Guiana. Pascal, their eldest son, had a fishing-line over the side, though he hadn't caught anything.

Peter streamed our trolling-line as we cleared the anchorage, and it snapped taut as we rounded the western headland. We discovered that he had hooked a small five-pound tunny, a species of tuna, when he hauled it alongside the boat; I leaned over and gaffed it with the new short-handled gaff that I had made while we were in Cayenne.

We had got used to catching and eating fresh fish, and we were now confident that we could hook a fish for dinner whenever we wanted, especially as we sailed along the fish-rich waters of the coast of South America. We hadn't always been so confident or such good fishermen when we first entered the Atlantic.

Before we left Canada I had clipped various magazine articles describing successful fishing rigs, tackle, and lures, but it was not until our passage from the Canary

Islands to the Cape Verdes that we began to catch fish regularly. As we sailed towards South America we perfected our technique.

Now, with his freshly hooked tunny flopping in the cockpit, our young but ever-eager fisherman again set out our 100 metres of 100-pound-test monofilament line; the swivel and two-foot-long wire leader ended in a red-and-white plastic octopus, the lure we found most successful. As soon as the line was out, I started to clean the tunny, slashing off thick fillets and then skinning them. I like to clean our catches right away to keep the boat sweet-smelling.

"Are there any eggs?" asked Penny, watching me as I slit the fish's guts open. The children are very fond of fish roe, especially when it's lightly fried with a touch of garlic as soon as the fish is cleaned.

"Not this time," I replied, throwing the carcass over the side to provide food for some predator. Then, with a few buckets of salt water and a scrub brush, I washed the cockpit clear of blood and scales. Meanwhile, Fiona soaked the fillets in a heavy brine solution, to bleach out the blood and the fish oil. I could hardly wait to roll the fillets in cornmeal and fry them in garlic and oil.

"Fish ho!" Peter shouted again as the old spear-gun rubber we use as a shock-absorber on the trolling-line stretched once more. Once again I pulled a little tunny over the rail, but this time I asked Peter to wind up the fishing-line onto our wooden reel, as we now had plenty of fish for the next two days. It was too late in the day to catch another fish and start drying it, because that needs hot morning sunshine.

As dusk fell, we angled away from the coast to sail past Surinam. In 1980 a military coup had ousted Surinam's elected government:

Parliament was dismissed, the constitution was suspended, and a state of emergency was declared. Two years later, fifteen opposition leaders were executed by the government of Colonel Bouterse, and anti-mercenary committees – vigilantes searching for suspicious persons – were set up throughout the country. We had hoped to visit Paramaribo, the capital and chief port, but current word on the yachting grapevine was to avoid Surinam.

Sadly, Guyana, the next country on this stretch of coast, was also to be avoided, according to rumour in our peripatetic community. It had not been long since the mass suicide of the James Jones religious sect had put Guyana in lurid headlines around the world, and the word was that the Guyanese government was, understandably, still not very welcoming to white North Americans.

We headed straight for the small, friendly island of Tobago, because, though we might be considered adventurous in terms of challenging Mother Nature, slow-moving yachts and yachtsmen are vulnerable when political storms brew, and we tend to avoid areas of unrest with as much care as we avoid hurricanes.

"That must have been a big one," said Peter, as our fishing-line snapped with a loud crack the next morning. "I think we've just lost our lure."

Peter, no matter what he is doing, keeps an ear cocked for the twang of the fishing-line shock cord. Occasionally something really big strikes, and stretches the two-foot-long shock cord to as much as ten feet before something snaps. At times the broken line lashes back like a whip and coils itself on the side deck. We then have to put on a new lure, a new leader, or even a whole new line.

But sometimes really big fish are landed by small yachts. One of our friends, Doug, a single-hander on the 27-foot British-registered *Loru*, told us the ultimate big-fish story. He sails with about seventy yards of 100-pound-test nylon line and a four-foot wire leader, using it as a hand line with no rod or reel. He hooked a seven-foot sailfish on a small octopus lure near the British Virgin Islands. As the line came bar taut, he knew he had

180

a big fish, but it wasn't until it leaped out of the water that he realized how big it was. It was too heavy to pull in while still fighting, so Doug, not knowing what else to do, just kept sailing to keep the line taut and to tire the fish out. It was not until an hour later that he hove to and began to try to haul the monster up to his stern. When he got it close and shot it with his spear gun, it began such frantic thrashing that it removed a few hunks of gelcoat from his hull. Possessed by a greater strength than he knew, Doug got the fish on board, but it continued to thrash about so much that he began to fear for his small fibreglass boat. In sheer desperation, he grasped the fish in a bear hug, and man and fish went down together for the fish's death throes, thrashing about in *Loru*'s tiny cockpit.

"I didn't know which one of us would give up first," said Doug. "I was bruised and limping around for a week afterwards."

Free-roaming ocean (pelagic) species of fish are always safe to eat. But in a coral area or around tropical islands some fish are toxic, bringing on ciguaterra-poisoning attacks, which can be fatal. The problem is that while some fish are commonly eaten with no problems in one area, the same species taken a few islands down the chain can be toxic. Barracuda, for instance, are reputed to be toxic in many areas in the Caribbean water north of Martinique, yet we ate a lot of barracuda all along the South American coast. Many people will not eat trigger fish, parrot fish, or any fish with a beak, as these coral-crunchers are more prone to carry ciguaterra, yet people on different islands eat these fish all their lives.

Our solution to this problem was a simple one: when spear-fishing or hand-lining in island reefs where we are suspicious of ciguaterra, we ask the locals if any fish are toxic and therefore to be avoided. We have never been given inaccurate information.

Though we were in the trade-wind area of the North Atlantic, the winds failed to blow with any conviction. We had been sailing slowly, with only forty-five miles on the log for the first twenty-four hours. Although the overcast skies prevented me from getting a celestial fix, I wasn't worried, as we were well offshore. Still, I was relieved that the following day was sunny enough for me to get both a morning and an afternoon sextant sight – even though the result astounded me. The entry for 1230 Saturday 18 August 1984, after two days of sailing, reads: Cel. fix 7°39′N, 55°16′W, miles on log 105 (since leaving Île Royale), miles over the bottom 216! Never before had we been carried so far and so fast by an ocean current. I was wary, and took more sextant sights that evening, but they confirmed our position. For the rest of the passage we took sights whenever we could, and kept a watchful eye on our position.

"Penny and Peter, come up and see the sharks!" I called out the next day. I had washed the morning dishes in the bucket in the cockpit as usual and then dumped the washing-up water over the side. As I did so, two sharks, each perhaps four feet long, dashed from their hiding-place beneath the hull to inspect the discoloured water for edible scraps. Satisfied that nothing they could eat had gone over the side, they returned to swim just under the turn of the bilge. Penny and Peter excitedly approached and peered over the gunnel, but, frightened by the size of the creatures, they jumped back into the cockpit. From there they once again peered over the side of the boat at the sharks, which were effortlessly keeping pace. We pulled in the trailing log line, lest they attack it; and the fishing-line remained on its reel in the cockpit, as I didn't want to stream it and risk catching a shark on the line.

The two predators kept pace with us throughout that day, and were still there the following morning. They raced out to inspect any scrap thrown overboard, taking only a couple of seconds to streak thirty or forty feet through the water. More than ever this wasn't the time for one of the kids to fall overboard! That night we sailed through a fishing fleet, and we were not sorry when our unwanted companions powered off to follow the fishing boats, where the pickings would surely be more generous.

The fishing-line had not been out too long when Fiona shouted "Fish ho!" She had been roused from her cockpit doze when the shock cord suddenly stretched. Now it was being pulled so hard that the line was flexing as it stretched far behind us, nearly stopping the slow-moving boat. Penny pulled in the log line as I donned my cotton gloves and prepared for a fight. We all gaped as we saw a five-foot-long dorado, flashing gold and blue, leap clear of the water and tailwalk on the surface as he thrashed his head to and fro. Suddenly the line went limp, as he successfully spat out the hook.

Fighting and landing these large game fish is a real thrill, and one I eagerly look forward to. For us it's become a common occurrence, while many city-dwellers pay hundreds of dollars a day just for the sight of such a fish. Fishing and yachting – not to mention good eating – do go together, but some caution is advised when fighting a large one, as the tale of Gregg Stokes shows. We had met Gregg and Patti Stokes and their two young daughters in Brazil after they had sailed their 35-foot cutter *Windsong of Knysna* across the South Atlantic. Gregg is a keen fisherman who had a socket for his heavy sport-fishing rod and reel at the pushpit at the stern of his yacht.

In mid-ocean, he hooked a large dorado just at dusk. *Windsong* was sailing along with the jib poled out, running before the southeast trades, steering herself with the aid of the wind-vane. Patti and the two girls, aged three and five, were below, getting the evening meal.

"I've got a beauty on the line, love," Gregg shouted down to his wife. "Don't open any tins. We'll have fish steaks for supper."

Patti finished what she was doing and it was five minutes later when she came up on deck – only to find the cockpit empty. Not only was there no fish, but there was no Gregg. Frantically Patti scanned the horizon but saw nothing. She quickly noted *Windsong's* course, got the pole off the jib, and started the engine. She then swung the boat back along the course *Windsong* had come, praying that her quick compass calculations were correct and that she would find her way back to Gregg. The light was already failing. She didn't have much time before it would be dark, and impossible to find anything on the ocean.

Meanwhile, Gregg was indeed in the water, hidden among the waves. He had been leaning against the yacht's opening pushpit gate as he swung his gaff at the struggling fish alongside. The latch on the gate had sprung and Gregg had shot through the open gate and into the water, too surprised to even cry out. He surfaced to see *Windsong* sailing out of his sight towards the sunset over the ocean swells. To make matters worse, the bloodied fish was thrashing against his legs as he clung to the rod and gaff, and he feared a shark attack. There was nothing he could do but tread water and hope that Patti would come on deck. It seemed a long time before, briefly lifted on the ocean swells, he saw *Windsong* coming towards him. Shouting and waving, Gregg was eventually sighted and hauled on board. He was still holding the rod and gaff. He then proceeded to land the fish, which he and Patti and the two girls ate for dinner later that night!

We had been keeping close to our rhumb line (the direct-line course to a destination) with the two-knot current taking us in the direction we wanted to go, but on our sixth day out we found ourselves fifty miles too far east. Outguessing variable ocean currents is a trial for any navigator. We hardened up to point southwest, assuming we would be swept north as we tried to estimate in which direction the current might take us. We were now in real danger of being carried right past Tobago.

At noon the following day I shot the meridian passage of the sun, calculating our latitude from the sun's highest angle above the horizon. It was another surprising celestial fix, leaving me to ponder the vagaries of currents, for the calculation now put us forty miles *west* of our rhumb line. Some time during the night we had broken from the grip of the current going northeast, only to be swept westward towards the Serpent's Mouth, the famous narrow straits between the southwest point of the island of Trinidad and the mouths of the Rio Orinoco, sometimes named the Columbus Channel after the first European to sail through these historic waters.

184

In the course of our Amazon visit Penny meets 128-year-old Maria
de Purifacio.

On the beach at Les Hattes in French Guiana, with grateful giant turtle friends.

Visiting the open market in Guiria, Venezuela, Penny and Peter wear pareos, cloth wrap-arounds.

Lorcha's famous galley, source of much contentment.

Some of that contentment, as the family enjoys a meal of freshly-caught Venezuelan lobster in the cockpit, protected from the sun by a bedsheet.

Reading a chart, and reading a book in the cockpit.

The children like to lend a hand, whether with the laundry (in Trinidad), or with gathering food supplies such as these conch shells (in Las Aves, Venezuela).

Penny and Peter having fun
in the cockpit – and having
a fresh-water shower at
Porvenir in the San Blas
Islands, just off Panama.

Fringed by thatched roofs, Fiona towers over the chief of Porvenir Island and his wife as she introduces Peter to their grandchildren.

We avoided the Serpent's Mouth, and that night as we tried to head northeast, we sailed past the offshore oil rigs dotted along the east coast of Trinidad. Sighting the twelve-mile range light on Galera Point, the headland at Trinidad's most northeasterly point, we realized the current was still pulling us west. With only twenty-four miles to go to Scarborough, Tobago, we started the engine for additional power to motorsail into the now brisk easterly trade winds and foul current. It was a hard twelve-hour slog, with the wind whipping spray over the length of our little boat as we inched our way along the coast. At 1500 hours we tied up along the seawall in the snug little harbour of Scarborough, at the first of our Caribbean landfalls.

MONEY AND MAIL

23

Discovered by Columbus in 1498, Tobago was at that time inhabited by Carib Indians. European settlement began in 1641 when two ships of settlers landed on the north side of the island, and Tobago was invaded by successive cycles of Dutch, French, and English fleets until in 1877 it was ceded in perpetuity to the British Crown. The island was amalgamated politically with Trinidad in 1888, the islands achieving independence in 1962. It is a small island with a mixed and friendly population, descended from black slaves and Indian plantation workers, and it was the first English-speaking country we had visited since leaving Canada.

As we lounged in *Lorcha*'s cockpit in Scarborough Harbour with a pile of new English paperbacks at our feet, Paul and I talked about how much we had learned since we set sail more than a year ago. Sailing, navigation, making a landfall, and dropping anchor were becoming second nature to us, but experience had also taught us how to better handle such mundane subjects as money and mail. Mundane or not, they are a necessary part of voyaging.

As far as money is concerned, long-distance cruisers fall into a number of different categories. A few are independently wealthy or have adequate retirement funds which finance their new lifestyle; others have saved enough money to cruise for a finite period; a third category, like Paul and me, have saved enough money

British Crown . . . cruising budgets . . . careful style . . . luxury items
. . . world inflation . . . bank accounts . . . professional accountant
. . . line of credit . . . replenishing funds . . . currency regulations . . .
credit cards . . . Poste Restante

for perhaps two years' cruising but would be supplementing their savings with other income; and the final category takes in those daredevil voyagers who leave with very little money, confident that their trade or professional skills will earn them enough money along the way to support themselves.

And how much does it cost to pay your way for a year's cruising? This is a very difficult question, as so much depends on your accustomed lifestyle, your personal needs, your ability to budget, the size of your boat, and the number of people travelling. In our first year of travel, we spent just under $10,000. But by contrast we have met North American couples who think nothing of a budget of $20,000, and a European single-hander who spent $2,500 annually. (Single-handers often eat on other people's boats!)

Our budget allowed us to live in comfortable if careful style, and I think we could have spent less money if we had felt the need to do so, as a good proportion of our budget was spent on film, film-processing, and postage. We shopped at the local markets, ate local foods, found our entertainment in the new friends we were meeting, both ashore and afloat, and only bought such luxury items as chocolate or canned roast beef when we were in a country where these items were reasonable or even cheap. Thus we bought wine in the Azores and Madeira, duty-free goods in the Canary Islands, and 20 kilos of fresh coffee in Brazil – where there's an awful lot of coffee – at the unbeatable price of $2 a kilo. Restaurant meals and bar drinks can really blow a hole in your budget, though the small cafés in the Azores provided splendid dishes for a very reasonable sum, and we also ate out a lot in Brazil. Cruising the

187

Atlantic taking the route we did, of course, is far cheaper than voyaging down the eastern seaboard of the United States and the Caribbean, a route where things tend to be more expensive along the way.

"And remember, we spent very little on boat maintenance in our first year," Paul reminded me. "And we're not going to escape world inflation, so we should probably think in terms of adding $1,000 to our budget every year."

Penny and Peter have learned the value of money and matter-of-factly recognize whether the family can afford things or not. Christmas and birthdays are a time for celebration and special meals, but Penny and Peter understand they will be getting only one present from their mum and dad; their grandmothers always remember them, and there is usually a package from Scotland from their Uncle Alastair and Aunty Gay. The children's voyaging upbringing has taught them to wax enthusiastic when they get a special treat – and not to whine when they have to do without.

When yachties and their children get together for a beach barbecue, those grilling fresh-caught fish cook right alongside the low-budget potato-and-vegetable eaters and the high-flying steak-sizzlers. We all share equally the blue waters, the golden sands, and the palm-fringed beaches.

How to organize a bank account and how to get more money when you need it are major considerations in international cruising – and it proved to be more complicated than we realized when we started.

Some yachties had an arrangement with an efficient bank manager to oversee their account, while others had their bank statements forwarded to a relative or a special friend. As our financial commitments were complicated by the fact that we had income cheques from newspapers and magazines, as well as income from the rental of our house, which also necessitated prompt payment of the monthly mortgage and annual insurance bills, we delegated a Toronto accountant to look after our financial affairs. As he was to have full control, he had signing powers for our current chequing account and we also gave him power of attorney (enabling him to sign legal papers), and Danny Baratz was worth his weight in gold. The longer we voyage, the more we appreciate that having a home-based professional accountant to handle our affairs was the right decision for us. We always knew how much money we had, as Danny would send us a full statement of all our debts and credits every six months. We simply could not have handled these matters efficiently ourselves while voyaging.

One other thing we did before leaving Toronto was to meet with our bank manager to arrange for a *second* chequing account. This was a line-of-credit account, a "magic" account on which we could write a cheque without actually having funds in the account. This gave us the freedom to write a cheque when we were not sure of the exact state of our current chequing account. Monthly statements on this second account also went to Danny so that he could pay debits promptly and not incur mounting interest charges, and keep our credit rating good.

We found there were many complications to replenishing funds directly from our bank. When we tried telexing or telephoning for funds, we learned that our bank was unwilling to accept such modern techniques, and required a written request with original signature before they would forward funds. We also assumed that the bank in Toronto would have its own correspondent bank in each country, but discovered that this was not so. When we wrote the bank from Madeira asking for funds to be telexed to Las Palmas (our next port), we found only a letter of inquiry waiting for us when we arrived. Our Toronto bank asked *us* to designate the particular bank in Las Palmas where we could accept funds.

I also assumed that we could get money transferred in the currency we preferred. The particular currency does not matter too much in countries that have a stable economy, as there we could usually exchange however much money we wanted into dollars. But it did matter in such countries as Brazil, whose currency was worthless outside the country. Brazil has strict regulations governing how many dollars you can buy to take out of the country, so you could be left with a pile of worthless

Brazilian money if you transferred cash into the country that you were not going to spend.

We found it best to discuss currency regulations with a local bank manager before we moved a finger to get money transferred into that country. Every nation has its own regulations for dealing with foreign currency, and the best rule is never to assume anything but to check carefully before each and every transaction you are thinking of making.

After much trial and error, we found that the best answer to the problem of money transfer was to carry a credit card. The most versatile of the cards we used was undoubtedly American Express. Its most useful feature for the cruising yachtsman is that you can cash $1,000 by writing a personal cheque (this was where our line-of-credit account came in useful) every twenty-one days at any American Express office or affiliated bank. In other words, if your cruising budget was around $12,000 a year, you could, in theory, keep yourself in cash just by using your American Express card. At any rate, we found that American Express had more offices and more affiliated banks in more countries than any other card. It's also well serviced; when our card expired in a small town in Brazil, we were able to get it renewed by writing to the American Express-affiliated bank in the next town en route. We collected our new card seven days later.

We met many cruisers who had left their country of origin after selling everything they possessed and joyfully throwing their credit cards away. Many of them were later to be found trying to reinstate their cards, partly because they had had similar banking experiences to ours, and partly because voyaging also means exploring. When you visit a new country where you can safely leave your boat, you may want to hire a car; this proves hard to do without a valid credit card. Another use, of course, is for the unplanned expense, such as our buying new fittings for *Lorcha* in Las Palmas, and the $1,500 cost of the family's Amazon River trip. So, even if you don't intend to use your card much, it can still be useful to have one with you – or preferably two, since different cards have different uses in different countries.

It is hard to decide how much money to carry with you, and in what currency. We started out with $1,000 U.S. in cash and $1,000 in travellers' cheques. We soon realized that this was not nearly enough, as we had to start negotiating for extra funds within two months of leaving. We now try to carry $3,000 U.S. in cash and $3,000 in U.S. travellers' cheques when we leave a major centre. We try always to arrange things so that our funds do not run below $1,000 on board the boat. We acquire major funds about twice a year – or work our trusty American Express card.

Getting one's mail is not quite as complicated as transferring money, but there are a few wrinkles to learn.

First of all, we soon found that it doesn't make sense to try to get mail every month. This puts too much strain on whoever is handling your mail, and it means you spend precious cruising time tracking down letters and packets. We psyched ourselves into expecting mail three or perhaps four times a year – and really enjoyed it when we got it.

One mistake we made early on was to give out two or more upcoming mailing addresses. This is a mistake, as voyaging plans tend to be fairly elastic and we often found ourselves spending longer than we had planned in one place and then perhaps cutting another destination from our itinerary. It's a real drag to have to go somewhere just to collect your mail.

All over the Atlantic we had our mail addressed to Poste Restante, c/o the Main Post Office, and found this general-delivery address most efficient. The only country where mail went missing at the post office was Brazil, although if we arrived a few weeks late at a destination, mail might have already been sent back to the sender, as the Poste Restante sections hold mail for only a limited period, about fourteen to thirty days. And missing mail was obviously a big disappointment for us on our travels; it was wonderful to be kept informed about life back in the "other" world.

191

TOBAGO, TRINIDAD, AND A CREW

24

Penny and Peter were delighted to be in an English-speaking country. At first they were surprised to find they could talk to so many people, but soon there was a crowd of chattering local children playing around *Lorcha* at the dock.

The children's special friend was a very pretty little Indian girl called Camille. Her father was a fisherman and her mother helped make ends meet with her small roti stall at the edge of the dock. As it was the school holidays, Camille didn't have much to do, and so she played with Penny and Peter every day. One morning when Penny and Peter were going to go swimming off the boat, Camille asked if she could go too.

"Can you swim, Camille?" I asked automatically.

"Of course I can swim," she said, her eyes flashing as she pulled off her clothes to show she already had on her swimming-suit.

I stayed in the cockpit to watch her go in. She went down the old tire ladder we use as a boarding-ladder, let herself go – and sank. I grabbed at the hand I could see groping for the top of the water and hauled her on board.

"Don't you ever tell anyone you can swim again," I said, shaken.

"I didn't know it was so deep," she wailed. "I can swim on the beach, really I can."

Whenever a new child swims off *Lorcha*, I always watch closely, just to find out for myself what his or her swimming strength is. Time and again I have discovered that boating parents can't be too careful. Camille was on the far side of *Lorcha* and could easily have drowned because no one on shore could see that side of the boat. We promised her that one day we'd go swimming on the beach with her, but though she was still welcome on *Lorcha*, it was on the understanding that she never went swimming again.

There was another incident with Camille that made us realize how careful you have to be in a different culture, where misunderstandings can arise very easily. I was quite sorry for the bright little girl, who was so much on her own that she spent every day with Penny and Peter, and usually ate lunch with us.

"We're going to miss you when you go," I said one day. "You fit in with the family so well we'd really like to take you to Canada to stay with us. What do you think, Camille?" I joked.

Next morning, Camille turned up with her mother.

"I understand from Camille that you'd like her to go to Canada with you," said her mother, smiling. "She's spent the whole night packing and I've been trying to explain to her that we must get her a passport first. We don't mind if she goes – it would be a great opportunity for her."

The invitation had, of course, never been serious, and I was aghast at the outcome of our joking conversation. It wasn't easy to find the right words to explain what I had really meant, and I cursed my clumsiness.

We had outfitted the family with masks, fins, and snorkels in the Canary Islands, where equipment is inexpensive, but it had lain unused in our lockers thus far. The weather had been too rough in the Cape Verdes and the waters too cloudy along the northeast coast of Brazil. But Tobago's Bucco Reef is known for prolific reef life, and it was the perfect place to fall in love with snorkelling.

We initiated the children to reef-fish by taking a fine glass-bottomed-boat tour of Bucco Reef, and then it was time for a swim in the shallow waters of the Nylon Pool, one-half mile off the beach, but only four feet deep, with very warm, crystal-clear water. Penny and Peter were thrilled with the colourful fishes and shouted through their snorkels at the wonder around them.

"I touched a fish," shouted our avid little fisherman. "If I catch some, can we keep them?"

But try though he might, he never could grab one of the little fish, which kept darting just out of his grasp.

Penny's excitement was in seeing a three-foot barracuda – which sent her scuttling back to the safety of Paul's arms.

Penny and Peter were both good swimmers and could swim independently in deep water. Now that they had discovered the joys of snorkelling, they donned their masks and fins whenever they were allowed to swim around *Lorcha*, which we had anchored in Store Bay, close to Bucco Reef and the clear waters of Pigeon Point.

The children had found a whole new area to explore in the underwater delights of the Caribbean, and needed some new reference books. We did have a fish book on board for identifying the species we might catch when fishing, but it did not show many of the colourful small reef varieties. Soon Jerry and Idaz Greenberg's *The Living Reef* became much thumbed and nearly worn out as the children tried to identify what they had just seen below the water's surface each time they went for a swim. We soon became used to hearing Penny expound to Peter,

"Did you see that neon goby swimming around that tiny juvenile yellowtail damselfish?"

Fiona and I couldn't have been more pleased with their growing knowledge. There is no better way to encourage

194

children in the use of reference books than to have them so curious about a subject that they can't wait to delve into a reference book's covers.

"Did you sail all the way from Canada in that?" came a voice close beside us as we lounged in the cockpit.

The voice proved to come from a swimmer, who proved to be Rob Matthews, a Welsh medical student who was doing his fifth-year eight-week medical elective in the hospital in Scarborough. We struck up a conversation and soon invited him and his colleague Kate, also a British medical student, on board for a chat.

Rob had done some sailing near his native Swansea and had chosen Tobago for his summer elective because he had hoped to do some sailing aboard cruising boats. But though he had been in Tobago for one month, we were the first cruising sailboat he had seen. When he spotted *Lorcha* dropping anchor in Store Bay, he immediately swam out to try to meet us.

We grew to like Rob and invited him and Kate back for lunch a few days later. At the lunch our conversation was interrupted by a shout from Penny as her mask fell overboard. In a flash, Rob was over the side. He caught the mask before it touched the bottom, and I began thinking.

Lorcha's bottom was very foul with marine growth, which had slowed us down on our sail from French Guiana to Tobago. The hull needed a good scrub, which was a tiring job when we were anchored in deep water. Here we had an enthusiastic if inexperienced sailor, a good swimmer, and someone, we quickly observed, who liked our two children.

"How would you like to exchange your services scrubbing the bottom for a weekend sail to Trinidad?" I asked, and was delighted by Rob's enthusiastic response.

Since *Lorcha* was a steel-hulled boat, we had no need to visit Trinidad's ever-flowing "Pitch Lake", but this remarkable natural phenomenon was used by many wooden ships of yore to caulk their timbers, including Sir Walter Raleigh's fleet in 1595. We wanted to visit Trinidad both to pick up mail, and to see if it still deserved its aboriginal name of Iere, Land of the Hummingbird.

And so it was the next afternoon, after doing their morning and early-afternoon rounds at the hospital, Rob and Kate swam out to *Lorcha* and set to with brushes and scrapers, while I moved the grab-rope around the hull from time to time. Apart from that, I sat in the cockpit under the awning, while Penny and Peter splashed around their new-found companions, probably hindering more than helping our medical assistants as they worked their way around and under the hull.

"We'll leave on Friday evening and sail overnight," I told them. "We should be able to spend Saturday in Scotland Bay and then we'll head for the Trinidad Yacht Club on Sunday."

Everybody agreed to the plan – but somebody forgot to order up the wind. The usual fresh trade winds had inexplicably died and the sea was flat calm, with perhaps two knots of wind. Rob was terribly disheartened that his expected brisk sail had turned into a slow seventy-mile powering trip. But we took turns hand-steering through the night, and he at least got a good look at the stars and some phosphorescent dolphin trails as they cavorted around during his nightwatch.

The anchor was hardly down in Scotland Bay in the early morning when Rob and Kate appeared in their swimming-suits.

"Mind if we jump in, Skipper?"

I hardly had time to reply before two splashes wet the decks. And with squeals of delight, Penny and Peter rushed to follow. Mama and Papa were never so energetic after an all-night sail!

With Penny and Peter so well occupied and looked after, Fi and I were able to have a short nap before we cleared the boat, put up the awning, and prepared breakfast without the children underfoot. Having crew looked better all the time.

Having new people on board was a treat for Penny and Peter, too, and that evening we had trouble getting the children to bed.

"Can we have just one more story, Rob?"

"Can we play just one more game, Kate?"

And who could deny them their extra time with new friends?

196

"Will you really still be here in the morning?" asked Peter unbelievingly as Rob eventually tucked him into his bunk.

We were sitting in the cockpit at the Trinidad Yacht Club on Sunday when Rob stopped fidgeting about and came out with it.

"Kate's returning to England right after our elective at the hospital is over," he said, "but I'll have a couple of weeks before I have to be back. Could I join you in Venezuela – or wherever you happen to be – for some more sailing?"

"How long would you have?" I asked.

"Well, if I can change my flight and stretch my time to arrive the day classes start," he rushed on, "it would be about four weeks. Gosh, I'd really love to come."

"You'd have to continue to sleep in the cockpit under the awning," I warned him. "And to leave most of your luggage somewhere and only bring a minimum amount, but – we'd love to have you join us. What do you think, kids?"

With a cheer from Penny and Peter, our pact was sealed. The experiment with crew would continue.

PESTS
ON BOARD

25

From the Trinidad and Tobago Yachting Association anchorage fifteen miles west of Port of Spain, we crossed the Gulf of Paria. On the way we sailed past the Dragon's Mouth – known and feared by seafarers like Columbus, Drake, Raleigh, and Orellana – where the outflow of the Orinoco River meets the tidal waters of the Caribbean, sometimes causing dangerous whirlpools. We gave that lot a wide berth, and entered Venezuela for the first time at Guiria, where we had *Lorcha* slipped and sandblasted.

We wondered if Rob would really make it to join us there. We were expecting him on Saturday, but had decided we would wait until the Monday before actually leaving – communications were difficult between Tobago and Venezuela, and it had been hard to confirm arrangements. But sure enough, there was Rob swinging up the dock – with Penny and Peter racing down to greet him and give him a big hug.

"Great going, Rob," said Paul. "Cast off the bowlines. We can get to Ensa Cariaquita before dark."

We would stay one night at this isolated anchorage on the south shore of the Peninsula of Paria before another day-sail to the offshore islands. It was cold and wet when we dropped anchor and Rob looked at the lashing rain.

Guiria sandblasting . . . Rob joins us . . . rat ho! . . . no cats . . .
rat patrol . . . the dispatch . . . roach ho! . . . health department . . .
mangroves and mosquitoes . . . sand flies and an icy glare . . .
tropical sun . . . cockpit dodger . . . awnings . . . forehatch cover . . .
aloe vera cactus . . . IAMAT

"Hey, Skipper," he said. "It's really very wet in the cockpit. Do you mind if I sleep on the cabin floor until it clears up?"

"First day aboard – and already he's making demands," joked Fi. "Of course you can sleep inside."

We were all drifting off to sleep, listening to the pounding rain, when Fiona felt something on her leg. First on the ankle, then farther up. Then definitely crawling over her knee. It felt heavy-bodied and, as realization dawned, she gave a yell.

"It's the rat. He's on board. He's in my bed!"

On a small boat lights can't be switched on quickly. I heard Rob leap to his feet and I fumbled for some matches, but by the time the lamps were lit, Mr. Rat had disappeared.

"Are you sure it was a rat?" asked Rob.

"If you suspect you have a rat on board and you positively feel four little legs and a heavy, stumpy body scurrying up your leg, you sure as hell don't think it was a bluebird," Fiona snapped.

We both knew it was a rat, because we had seen one the day before. We had been tied alongside an old government tug in Guiria after we had finished painting the boat and were waiting for Rob. At about nine o'clock in the evening, I had gone on deck to get some fresh air and had noticed a large rat near our forehatch. I ran towards him and he jumped back onto the tug, which was probably his home. Immediately I got out all our screens and blocked off the vents, hoping another rat had not already found its way below. Now this.

We all went back to our sleeping-spots – but not to get much rest, as we heard the rat scrambling about and occasionally gnawing on food, or perhaps chewing a passage hole in the bulkheads. At one point I saw him as he scrambled over the spice bottles. He was a large, brown one – but at least he looked healthy!

In the morning we found other evidence of his presence. Both a plantain and an avocado had bites out of them. Mr. Rat was making himself right at home.

We couldn't do much about the rat that day as we had no trap or poison on board, but we reckoned the next night would not be too much of a problem as we were doing an overnight sail to the Testigos Islands and the movement of the boat would keep the rat quiet. So off we set – with many jokes at Fiona's expense. She took it well – but only on the condition we did our best to get rid of the rat as soon as we got there.

But the Testigos were inhabited only by a few fishermen and there was no place to get a trap.

"Let's see if anyone has a cat," said Fiona, so off we set to row around the six yachts in the anchorage. The Swedish schooner *Yawim* did have one, but unfortunately she was only six months old, and the children were afraid their young cat would be no match for a full-grown wharf rat. And I can't say I blamed them.

"Surely you two grown men can get rid of one small rat," said Fiona, a trifle unreasonably. "I don't care how you do it. It has to go."

So Rob and I devised a plan, eagerly aided and abetted by Penny and Peter. We put all the fruit, vegetables, and other vulnerable foods in the dinghy, which floated astern. We put in the screens, closed the main hatch, and blocked all the vents and locker lids so that the only opening from below to the deck was the forehatch. I then made a rough ramp up to this opening with some coils of rope and put a partly rat-eaten loaf of bread just outside on the deck.

We propped the hatch open with a stick, with a string around it leading along the deck to where Rob would stand watch.

"Is Rob staying on deck by himself?" whispered Penny.

"Why can't I pull the string?" demanded Peter.

But it was bed as usual for the kids – and as soon as it was dark, Fiona stretched out uneasily on her bunk. One lamp was dimly glowing. I lay on my bunk with flashlight in one hand, club in the other, and my eyes wide open.

As soon as the boat got quiet, the rat started to stir. I spotted him heading for the galley, and chased him towards the forehatch brandishing my club. A few minutes later he made another attempt towards the galley, but again I headed him off, forcing him back to the forecabin.

Suddenly there was a crash and the forehatch fell. The rat was now trapped on deck, unable to get back below.

"Stay in your bunks," I hissed to Penny and Peter as two heads appeared from two bunks while I took a flying leap up the companionway, carefully closing it behind me.

"Did you hear a splash?" I asked Rob urgently. "Did he jump overboard?"

"No, he's still around," said Rob. "But I can't see him."

After checking the water around the boat to be sure, we began to search the deck systematically, starting at the bow. We carefully moved all the clutter and looked into the vent boxes, working our way to the cockpit. There was no sign of the rat.

At the very end of our cockpit I have partitioned off a section where the propane gas bottles are installed. This is vented out the transom, so no gas leaks can get below. As I eased the locker door open by the light of Rob's flashlight, I saw the rat dive under the grates that held the gas bottles. He hid under a bottle and lay still – but his long tail gave away his exact position.

"Quick," I hissed to Rob. "Get me the fish-knife and the sheath knife by the companionway."

With one knife I pinned him down to the cockpit sole and with the other I skewered him, which was ghastly, because he shrieked for about thirty seconds, sounding just like a child. We watched the limp body disappear astern, and then sat in the cockpit for a celebratory drink, telling each other our parts of the successful hunt.

201

To our relief, there was only one rat, as our following nights of uninterrupted sleep testified.

"Roach!" Peter would shout, much to our embarrassment if we had guests on board. Then there would be much swatting and shuffling about and soon a "Got 'im" or a "He got away" would be announced to all within hearing. Though we managed to keep these pests off the boat for many months, by the time we were cruising the coast of Brazil, we had quite a few on board.

We always picked through our fruit and vegetables carefully as soon as we brought them on board. No cardboard cartons or paper bags were kept longer than to unload their contents. Egg cartons especially were examined and sprayed or thrown away, but still cockroaches came on board.

We sprayed around the galley with various bug bombs, such as Baygon, which seemed universally available and somewhat effective. But we were not to get rid of our roach population until we reached Bonaire, where for $20 the health department sent a professional on board to spray our boat with a powerful liquid.

But though the population is under control, the war still goes on. Common yachtie knowledge says:

"If you see one roach, you have ten. If you see two you have a hundred. If you see three, you have an infestation."

"Go right up near that island with the mangroves" are often the directions. "Drop anchor and you will be well protected, with lots of fish and conchs right below you."

The anchorage may be ideal – but mangroves usually mean mosquitoes and gnats. A sandy beach at your bow probably also means sand flies and gnats. Many harbours have a fish market nearby – great for fish but often terrible for flies.

All this means that screens are a necessity on cruising boats. We have screens built into all the vent boxes, rigid framed screens for the fore- and mid-hatches, and mosquito netting to hang over the companionway.

We also carry lots of bug repellent, not only to apply to our skins, but also to spray around the screens and mosquito nets to help keep the bugs away. Bug-free anchorages or marinas are few and far between, though with some protection we have found that it has never been a big problem.

"Look at these bites," said Fiona. "What do you think they are?"

Fiona should be hired to test insect repellents. For no matter where we are, there seems to be something that bites her. I am just the opposite; bugs seem to avoid me, obviously preferring Fiona's feminine blood.

But this was a real puzzler. There were no mosquitoes around our marina in Las Palmas, Gran Canaria. Neither the children nor I had been bothered by bug bites. But every morning Fiona would have large red welts. She would apply various repellents night after night, but to no avail.

"I wonder if it's a flea?" she suggested.

Our children had spent a lot of time playing with some other boat children who had both a cat and a dog on board. But the pets had never been on our boat, and the children had had no problem. As tactfully as possible, Fiona broached the subject with the children's father.

"Do you often buy bananas here?" was his reply.

It seems there is a kind of flea which lives on stalks of bananas in the Canary Islands.

"Soak your bananas in a bucket of water before bringing them on board," he said. "Any fleas will drown and float to the top of the water."

Well, that was a new one for us, but we decided to soak Fiona's sheets and blanket in a big bucket.

"Papa," said Penny. "I think there is a bug floating in the bucket with Mama's bedclothes."

I went to look and, sure enough, a sort of large flea was floating lifelessly on the surface of the water. I plucked it out on the tip of my finger.

"Fi, look at this," I said, bringing it near the companionway for her to see.

As Fiona approached, the dead flea revived itself, and made a mighty leap in Fi's direction, disappearing down the companionway into the boat's interior.

There was a terrible silence.

I have never before or since seen Fiona give such an icy glare. I apologized profusely, trying to counter some truly horrible threats, and thereafter took it upon myself to soak all bananas lest any of those threats ever be realized.

The sun, though not exactly a pest, can cause real discomfort. Cruising boats usually head for the sun and warm weather, but even the hardiest sun-worshipper cannot take constant exposure. Fortunately we had a larger than usual cockpit dodger made for the *Lorcha*. It was very welcome on the colder passages, and we found that even in the tropics we always sail with it up, and with the forward windows unzipped and rolled up to allow for some air circulation. And it afforded welcome shade while sailing. If we had had a larger boat, I would definitely also have had a Bimini Top made. For in the tropics you can surely have too much sun, but never too much shade.

In port we put up a large awning the width of the boat that shades *Lorcha*'s deck from the mast right aft to over the pushpit. In the rainy reason it keeps the rain out of the midships hatch as well as keeping the cockpit relatively dry. The shade it gives keeps the cabin cool and protects those having a nap in the cockpit, where the trade winds make midday napping a sweatless pleasure.

Our awning is made from a medium-weight cotton canvas with grommets to tie it to the lifelines and a few wooden battens to spread it to full width. Though we often see awnings with roll-up sides, they are seldom used and seem an unnecessary complication. They also restrict air flow and make the cockpit rather airless.

When making your awning, give some thought to incorporating a raincatcher. A hose fitting installed where the awning sags, or a gutter to collect the runoff, can save you a lot of time lugging jerry cans, and you don't ever have to worry as to whether it is safe to drink or not.

Another bit of canvas that I sewed up was a cover for the forehatch, so that it could be left open when it was raining hard, to prevent our main salon from becoming uncomfortably hot. Though it took a bit of experimentation as to the necessary shape and positioning, it was a worthwhile addition.

We carry many sun-screen lotions as well as sunburn ointments, but the best cure for sunburn is still prevention. Though we try to keep Penny and Peter covered up when they are playing on the beach, they do occasionally get a painful burn. To fix that, the Swedish schooner *Yawim* gave us a small aloe vera cactus growing in an old coffee tin. It lives under the forehatch, getting some sun and plenty of fresh air, and happily sprouts new leaves with the bi-monthly sprinkling of water it receives. When the children get a burn, we break off a small segment of a mature leaf and smear the inner pulp on the sunburned skin. The pain is immediately relieved, and by the next day the children are ready again for a good play on the beach.

Though the cruising life is a healthful one, one does occasionally want to consult a doctor in some far-flung corner of the world. When we are in a major city, we call the Canadian, U.S., or British embassy or consulate to ask for the name of a good local doctor. But we have been impressed by the services of the International Association for Medical Assistance to Travellers (IAMAT), an association geared to providing world travellers with information on malaria and other diseases, and on the safety of local foods and water, as well as a list of English-speaking doctors trained in North America or Britain who are familiar with the medicines and medical needs of North American voyagers. A third alternative is the out-patient department of the local hospital; but staying healthy is always better than even the best care.

VENEZUELAN
AMBASSADORS

26

The Testigos were the first of the Venezuelan offshore islands we were to visit. All are sparsely inhabited, with only a few fishermen and their families, or are completely deserted. There are no stores, and often no fresh water is available.

But Testigo Grande had marvellous sandy beaches, as well as large sand dunes. Our children soon became friends with the three children on *Yawim* (a Swedish-registered schooner built in the United States and owned by Ricco, an Italian, and his wife, Gitta, who was Swedish), and there was much playing about on the beach as well as other outings which included all five children. Our little eight-foot dinghy is a good carrier, but with Rob, Fiona, and me, as well as five children, it strained her capacity. At least it wasn't far to the shore and there was no surf.

But how we loved the Testigos! Rob found his first lobsters here, and one afternoon collected six within about an hour. Spear-fishing wasn't too good close in, however, as the waters were routinely fished and the locals were also well equipped with snorkelling gear.

"Can I buy some fish?" I asked a local fisherman one day, as he was loading a huge catch into his refrigerated hold.

"Choose what you like," he replied, first in Spanish, and then in French when he realized I spoke French; he

Lobsters . . . fish gift . . . the curious barracuda . . . Isla Margarita
. . . oysters . . . Canadian Embassy . . . medal for goodness . . .
Los Roques . . . almost aground . . . Los Aves . . . conch

transported fish from the Testigos north to Martinique for the market there.

I chose two fat snappers from a basket on his deck.

"What do I owe you?" I asked, taking out my wallet.

"Put away your money," he replied. "We have a tradition here – if you want fish for your family to eat, they are free. I would only charge you if you wanted them for resale."

One afternoon I watched an unusual form of fishing. Five young men appeared in a fishing boat. Three of them went into the water with their masks and snorkels, and began swimming around in ever-decreasing circles. The remaining two men in the boat spread a net around outside the three in the water. Then the three swimmers climbed aboard and all five men hauled in the net. They had captured about thirty barracuda averaging 24 inches (60 cm) each.

"The barracuda are curious and territorial," a fisherman busy cleaning his catch explained to me. "They'll gather around a swimmer to see what he's about. We cast the net around everyone – and get a good catch. Of course, you have to know where the barracuda are in the first place. Would your kids like to help us?"

Although they claimed no one had ever been attacked by the barracuda, we declined their invitation. Maybe when they were a little older . . .

Rob had brought a stunt kite out from England with him, and we often flew it on the beach and among the sand dunes. It was great fun, especially when it attracted a flock of curious frigate birds, which tried to follow the kite's swoops and spins.

It was with reluctance and only when our fresh water and other supplies had begun to run low that we headed west to the larger island of Isla Margarita. This is a populous island and a duty-free port, though not a very inexpensive or well-stocked one. But ice was cheap and easily obtained and a case of beer cost only about $4.50. We anchored off the Concorde Hotel, just off a fine beach, and to our delight met up with cruising friends we had not seen since Brazil and French Guiana. Just like old-home week!

Soon Fiona and Rob were diving for oysters. We had seen the local fishermen diving for them only a few hundred yards off the beach. We had mentally marked a seemingly popular spot, and decided to try our luck when they moved on. With the water only about fifteen feet deep, Fi and Rob quickly had a couple of bucketfuls, and we shared them around the anchorage. Cold beer and fresh raw oysters with crackers and Tabasco sauce. That's living.

Rob began borrowing a windsurfer from Rick on *Donnerdag*, a Belgian boat we had met in French Guiana, and was soon giving Penny and Peter rides on the back, as well as teaching Fiona how to sail it.

But Rob's time with us was all too soon over. When he left, we made up a list of things we needed from England and asked him to mail them to us. We bade him a very fond farewell, for he had truly become a member of the family; more than a year later, Peter was still asking when we would see his friend Rob again.

La Tortuga, the next island to the west, was reputed to have better diving for fish and lobster than Margarita, but we found it only notable for its airport. We had hardly dropped anchor when we heard a light aircraft buzz the beach and then come in to land. As soon as he had cleared the sand runway, another, and then another, landed. I counted seventeen single-engined aircraft coming in that Saturday morning. It seemed that the island was a popular destination for wealthy picnickers from Caracas. There were only a few beach huts and perhaps ten fishermen's families living there occasionally, but the unattended runway was a busy one. The beach was also littered with the wreckage of light aircraft, so all flights were not successful.

It was not a long passage from La Tortuga to Puerto Azul and Venezuela's capital city, Caracas – in miles, that is. But there was certain to be a great difference in our lifestyle, if only for four days. For during our stay in the huge modern city of Caracas, we were to be guests at the Canadian Embassy.

One of the fleet in which we sailed down the St. Lawrence in 1983 was the Ontario 32-foot sloop *Esmeralda*, captained by Jim Midwinter with his wife Sally. We didn't know it at the time, but our genial companion was none other than the ambassador-designate for Venezuela. While we had been sailing around the Atlantic, his ambassadorship had come through, and he had invited us to come and stay with him. We were eager to meet the Midwinters again. We wanted to hear about their trip from Newfoundland, where we had last seen them, and they were curious about our travels around the Atlantic.

Describing the functions of an ambassador to Peter was rather like the occasion when we had prepared the children to meet Toronto's Mayor, Arthur Eggleton, for the first time. After hearing a long list of the Mayor's responsibilities and duties, Peter understood.

"You mean, he's the king," he said.

This visit ashore was serious business, and Penny and Peter treated it as such.

"It's all right to spit over the side when we're on the boat, Peter, but it's not polite to spit in embassies," was Penny's contribution.

Peter worried about his sartorial elegance.

"Do children at embassies wear knickers?" he asked. (It's often so hot on board the kids don't put on underwear.)

But if the thought of staying with almost-royalty had put the children somewhat in awe, the imposing colonial-style Embassy itself did not alarm them one whit. The beautifully appointed twenty-room mansion was surely the biggest house they had ever stayed in, but thanks to the Midwinters, its sustained cool elegance was also full of warmth. The parents of three grown children themselves, Jim and Sally simply took the children in their stride.

Too many cockroaches and too little fresh water on board *Lorcha* gave rise to the following diplomatic conversations in the Embassy:

"Jim, would you like my bottle caps to help catch roaches?" said Peter.

"Sally, shall I save the bath-water for laundry?" asked Penny.

Having slept in narrow bunks within arm's length of each other for sixteen months, both children elected to sleep in separate bedrooms. Both rooms had a chest of drawers and a desk, and Penny, often an untidy monkey on board, neatly folded away all her clothes and set her Grade 2 work in orderly piles in the desk drawers. That gave Jim an idea.

"Would Penny and Peter like to go to school for the day?" he asked. "We could probably fix it up with the English School here."

I said yes before I had thought it through and asked the children, but luckily they were both keen. We were surprised by Peter's reaction, because when he attended nursery school in Canada, starting back at school after a couple weeks' holiday had always been a traumatic experience for him.

It was typical of Jim's kindness and understanding that even after a very late night at an official reception, he was up at 6:30 in the morning because he thought someone should personally introduce the children to the school. All went extremely well. Armed with a map and several photographs, the children gave a talk to their classmates at school. They must have made an impression.

"The English School will never be the same after the visit of Penny and Peter," said headmistress Catherine Judge. "All the children want to go sailing."

During our busy four days at the Residence, Jim and Sally also gave a dinner reception in our honour and asked us to do a slide show of our travels. Thoughtfully, they organized the invitation so that it said "dress informal".

After their triumph at school, the kids scored high with the Ambassador, too. "A 'Medal for Goodness', Mama," gasped Peter, his eyes sparkling with excitement as Jim placed a gold medal with red, white, and blue ribbon around his neck, and gave Penny an impressive pewter medallion. The wily Ambassador had not only given infinite pleasure to our two youngsters – but shrewdly ensured the impeccable behaviour of both of them at any embassy they might visit in future years.

Meanwhile, we took full advantage of the chance to see one of the great cities of the world. By the time Simon Bolivar, "The Liberator", was born here in 1783, the locally born Spaniards, the mixed-blood Mestizos, and the Carib and Arawak Indians were irked by rigid rule from Spain. After a series of bloody uprisings, independence from Spain was declared here in 1811 – and nine months later the city was destroyed by an earthquake. The continuing war devastated the country and killed more than twenty-five per cent of the population until independence was established in 1823, with Caracas continuing as the capital of the new country, and Bolivar continuing in his quest to liberate the rest of South America.

After oil was discovered in 1914, Venezuela became the richest country in South America, with the highest per-capita income. This is a situation that is changing today as oil prices drop, but the city of Caracas, built on hills that mark the northern end of the Andes chain, is still a very impressive sight.

But after four days of daily hot showers, wonderfully served meals, spirited conversation, and elegant surroundings – not to mention visits to the city, its huge buildings a legacy of the oil boom of the 1950s – it was time to return to our thirty-foot home and head offshore again.

Venezuelan sailors had told us we had to visit Los Roques, a group of islands about seventy miles offshore. We knew that the currents off the top of South America can run very strong, up to three knots westerly, or weakly to the east. So, after being assured that the current was very weak, we set sail as the sun went down, hoping to reach the eastern entrance of Los Roques just after dawn. With a twenty-knot wind just forward of the beam, and allowing for the current, it should have been a fast and easy sail.

But at dawn there was nothing in sight. We had run our distance, and should have been well within sight of Los Roques, whose low coral reefs spread across nearly thirty miles from east to west.

I tried to get a fix using the radio direction-finder, but couldn't make sense out of it, so we turned west, thinking we had perhaps over-compensated for the current and lay too far east. I also got out the sextant and took a sight. We jilled about, not sure what to do in these reef-strewn waters, though there was perfect visibility. By the time I could get a second sextant sight to cross the two lines of position to get a position fix, it was late afternoon and we found we were far to the northwest of the group.

The "weak" current must have carried us to the northwest at nearly three knots during the night, sweeping us past the western end of the group before dawn. Only with great luck had we avoided coming to grief on the reefs during the hours of darkness.

Now that we knew (or thought we knew) where we were, what to do? Trying to get back to the group would be a hard, rough sail and one I had no wish to do. So we gave up on Los Roques and hardened up on the port tack, hoping to sight the light of the Aves group, which lay further west, during the night.

About midnight, I sighted a light. All marine lights, of course, flash a distinctively timed signal, and as we approached we timed the sequence to be that of the light at the west end of the Roques group. This didn't make sense, unless we were really lost; so we sailed to within a few miles of the flashing beacon and then hove to until dawn.

All the lights in these groups were on metal-framework towers, so studying the beacon in daylight was no help.

"I'll head up towards it slowly," I said to Fiona. "We'll treat it as the western end of Los Roques – but we'll go carefully."

As we looked for a passage, the water suddenly shoaled and turned light blue.

"Turn around, Fi. Turn around," I shouted to Fi on the helm.

Luckily we were going very slowly and Fiona responded immediately, but nevertheless we gently touched a coralhead, which made me glad that we weren't trying this in the dark.

212

"Let's head round the other side and get a bearing on the outer islands to see if it matches with Los Aves de Barlovento," Fiona suggested. "It can't be Los Roques because of the shoalling here, so it must be one of the Aves."

I squinted into the hand-bearing compass as we rounded the sand spit with the light on it. "Okay – that means it must be the Aves de Sotovento. Keep as you're going."

We looked at the chart and everything seemed to match, with a safe anchorage showing just behind the spit. We dropped anchor in the clear water of a gently shelving beach. I was about to go below to get the sextant to take another series of sunsights when a fast boat appeared round the end of the island.

"Welcome to Los Aves de Sotovento," said Bartholomew, only resident and representative of the Guardia Nationale on these Venezuelan islands.

At least our mystery was solved, but as we sat in the cockpit chatting with him, I asked Bartholomew about the light. He shrugged his shoulders expressively.

"Sometimes it flashes once every nine seconds. Sometimes once every six," he said, and then paused. "And sometimes it doesn't flash at all!"

The Aves group was the best place we had seen for variety and abundance of coral-reef life. The diving was superb, and fish, lobster, and conch were plentiful. Even when we weren't searching for food, we were delighted with the wonder of the colourful life around us. We changed anchorages several times, and found something interesting at each. What made it all the more wonderful is that we saw the most beautiful live coral and fish in depths of four to seven feet of water, which meant that Penny and Peter were able to go everywhere with us.

We didn't let them wander too far on their own, though, because we soon found that every reef was guarded by its own very large barracuda. Often, when we were swimming in a new reef, a 6-foot monster would swim out to give us the once-over. Their usual pattern was to circle us twice and then swim off, and we soon got used to them and ignored them. My thinking was that, as Fiona and I were roughly their size, it was a stand-off, but I didn't want our smaller and more vulnerable children to be around these large ugly-looking fish on their own.

One day when I was hauling up a bucket of sea water to wash the dishes, I found a tiny one-inch-long octopus in it. I called the children and fetched him out on my fingertip.

"See how he's changing colour," I explained as he went from brown to pink to a mottled combination that he thought suited my finger. "That's how this baby hides from a big fish that might eat him."

We put him in a fresh bucket of sea water for further observation before returning him to his home territory. That territory proved to be the first place where Penny and Peter could actively participate in foraging for food underwater.

"Papa. Papa. I found this one all by myself," shouted Peter as he struggled to keep his head above water while holding a conch so large it needed both his hands.

And soon we depended on the children to search for these beautiful, but vulnerable, pink shellfish to make delicious conch fritters. They were so plentiful that Peter and Penny could quickly find six or seven good-sized ones diving in only four to six feet of water.

But it was now December, and time to be moving on. We wanted to respond to an invitation we had received to Christmas dinner eighteen months prior, and we wondered if the Johnsons of Kralendijk, Bonaire, were still expecting the sailing family they had never met!

BOUNTIFUL BONAIRE

27

W e hadn't quite made a full circuit around the Atlantic Ocean, but our lives were coming full circle in another way. When we first left Canada, I had written an article for the *Toronto Star* telling about our background and proposed voyage. Among the countries I said we hoped to visit were the Netherlands Antilles.

A copy of that article had found its way down to two Canadians, Keith and Barbara Johnson in Kralendijk, the capital of Bonaire in the Netherlands Antilles. And Barbara immediately wrote to us care of the *Star* to invite us to spend Christmas 1983 with them "if you get that far."

Now at Christmas a year later we were taking them up on their invitation. Fortunately, Keith and Barbara had been receiving copies of our *Star* articles from home, so they were not in the least surprised when we called them from the Bonaire Marina in early December after a day-sail from the Aves. Keith wheeled up to *Lorcha* in his truck about five minutes later.

"Hello, Peter. Hello, Penny," he said. "We're still expecting you for Christmas dinner, you know. Christmas here is a bit different from Canada. How would you like to go snorkelling on Christmas Day?"

When Bonaire was discovered in 1499 by Amerigo (as in America) Vespucci, it was then populated by a tribe of Arawak Indians, the Caipuetos, who were still living in

Christmas invitation . . . marine park . . . Dee Scarr . . . "Touch the Sea" . . . feeding fish . . . Dee's fish family . . . "Number One" . . . fish-cleaning stations . . . friendly scallop . . . octopus overture . . . Moray eels . . . Peter's pet

---

the Stone Age. They were soon wiped out in the usual round of piracy and other larceny, and the Dutch took over the island in the early seventeenth century, primarily attracted by the salt pans there. But the major influx of settlers were Jews from Spain and Portugal fleeing the Spanish Inquisition. It was this mix of settlers who created papiamento, the unusual lingua franca of the Dutch Islands.

Bonaire is the smallest of the three islands that make up the Dutch "ABC" islands – Aruba and Curaçao are the other two – but it is the one that is the best-known to the diving community. More than a decade ago the sea around the island was declared a marine park, and the diving sites and opportunities are nothing less than spectacular; the water can be crystal-clear with from fifty to one hundred feet of visibility, depending on weather conditions.

But what made our stay on Bonaire quite extraordinary was meeting Dee Scarr, who runs a program called "Touch the Sea". She was strolling down the docks where *Lorcha* was moored when she tripped over a fishing-line Peter had out.

"Hello," she said to Peter. "Where are you from, and why are you tripping up people on the dock? Don't you know you should be feeding fish and not catching them?"

I came up on deck to see what the problem was and in no time Dee was sitting on board and we were exchanging stories.

"Do you mind if I take your kids out snorkelling?" she said. "They really should be meeting more fish. Come on, Penny and Peter, I'll take you to a special place."

217

We hadn't a clue what Dee was talking about, but Penny and Peter will go snorkelling anywhere with anybody, and off went the three musketeers. What followed was probably the most extraordinary experience of Penny's and Peter's lives.

Donning her mask and snorkel, holding a plastic container of food – hot dogs, for heaven's sake – Dee swam off closely followed by our two moppets. Arching her back and flicking her feet up in the air, she plunged underwater and sat on the shallow sandy bottom, where she opened her food box. Breaking off small bits of hot dog, she waved them around – and within seconds was surrounded by fish eating out of her hands! Wrasses, angelfish, damselfish, yellowtails, and others flocked around her.

The kids, lying on the surface of the clear water with their masks on, could see everything. Dee demonstrated once or twice for them and then, swimming to the surface (the water was only six to ten feet deep in the spot she had chosen), she motioned for the kids to take a piece of hot dog and do the same thing. Even though they could not sit on the bottom or stay underwater as long as Dee, they could feed the fish. *Never had any of us seen fish so tame.*

One reason the fish are so tame lies in the ecology and reef management here. Through some very far-sighted thinking and planning, ten years ago the waters around Bonaire were declared a national park, and spear-fishing was outlawed. The fish here have nothing to fear from the odd two-legged humans swimming amongst them, and divers soon developed the habit of hand-feeding them. It was all new to us, however, and it was hard to believe this extraordinary sight.

"The fish actually swim towards you," said Penny afterwards. "They come up to take the food, and some of them actually seem to nuzzle you."

"It's a funny feeling when the fish takes the food," said Peter, giggling. "The fish sort of bites your finger – and it sort of tickles. It doesn't hurt a bit."

It was not until we got to know Dee better that we realized that she was not totally our discovery, but that this extraordinary personality is gaining an international reputation for her abilities to communicate with sea creatures. Her natural sympathy and empathy with them, along with hours of study, enable her to swim with them, feed them, play with them, fondle them, and, above all, add to the world's scant fund of knowledge about the habits of underwater creatures.

Her insightful book *Touch the Sea* documents these experiences and tells the stories of the lives of fishy friends whom Dee regards as family – fish like the little red hind she calls Darling, the grouper named Falstaff, Oliver Twist the Flounder, and Friday the filefish, to name a few. Dee writes about getting to know these fish, learning their habits and foibles, and swimming and having fun with them for months and, in some cases, years. They become such friends that when a fish no longer appears – presumably having died or been eaten – Dee writes about feeling a personal loss.

In *Touch the Sea*, Dee writes:

> Darling, Friday, Oliver Twist, Adelle Davis, Popcorn, King Midas, so far these are the only members of my undersea "family", but our interactions have taught me that the possibility for friendship with marine creatures has no limit. I dream of someday having my "own" reef, one which no one dives without me. What an incredible opportunity that would be, to explore further how relationships can develop between diver and marine animal.

It was an extraordinary lesson in communication for all of us, but in particular for Penny and Peter. I don't know how their lives are going to develop, but it was from this time on that Penny started talking about becoming a marine biologist, and Peter more than ever began to feel in tune with the life of the sea.

But snorkelling was just scratching the surface of Dee's experience, and I arranged to do a couple of underwater scuba dives with her, promising to tell Penny and Peter all about it. We went to the old pier at Kralendijk, a habitat known well by Dee, as she was on her 306th dive there.

"Number One", the first Moray eel Dee usually visits, was not in his usual place, so we swam over to some gently waving sea anemones, growing at a depth of about twenty feet. First Dee showed me how to let the anemone gently cling to my fingers and pull them under. This creature looked like a plant – but it ate like an animal and was soon sucking on the small bits of hot dog Dee offered it. And Dee knew exactly where the spotted cleaner shrimp would be on the anemone's waving tentacles and she gently plucked him out and set him on my fingers. He assumed that I, too, wanted cleaning and went at my nails in good style!

By this time an angelfish had come around, and was trying to attract Dee's attention. I could almost hear her saying, "Here, sweetie," as she opened her can of food and held out a hot dog.

A group of grunts swam up, and this time I also got to offer them some hot dog. In and out the fish darted, whacking off quite big pieces of the hot dog. It was noticeable, however, that they much preferred to take food from Dee than from me.

A scallop in a saucer-shaped shell was our next creature. Dee held it on her hand and suddenly the shell opened. There was just enough time for us to see beautiful fringes and blue spots inside before she swam off, looking like a Spanish castinet as she opened and closed her shell through the water.

Though Dee goes back again and again to visit the creatures under the pier, she's never bored. She can give people an interesting dive because she knows where all the creatures are, but for her the excitement is that on almost every dive something new will happen.

Take the octopus. He lived in an old pipe, an empty crab-shell and other refuse at the entrance giving away his presence. Dee was pleased to see him back, as he hadn't been there all week. Spontaneously she gave him one of her diving-gloves and he eagerly took it. Lying on her stomach, Dee eased back a few feet to see what he would do next. He pulled the glove into his pipe and then, for the first time, came all the way out. He seemed to hesitate and then swam for Dee's hand, which was resting on the sand. To our utter astonishment, he curled his tentacles round

220

her fingers and led her – at least her hand – into his house! Some extraordinary barrier had been broken, and the octopus was clearly making friends.

Dee was still bemused as we swam over to some tires at the end of the pier and, now thirty feet under, she opened her food box and took out some raw fish. This was the signal for "Mr. Greedy", the Moray eel she's been befriending for two years, to come out.

A word about Moray eels. They grow to about 6 feet and have mean faces. Their wide jaws open and close menacingly as they swim around you. Their teeth are extremely sharp and they can take several hunks out of your flesh with no bother at all. They are regarded as dangerous reef predators, and most divers avoid them.

Yet here was three-and-a-half-foot Mr. Greedy rubbing himself against Dee's wet-suit and allowing Dee to stroke him under the chin. He's learned some manners over the years and says hello before he gets offered any hot dog or fish.

Miami-born Dee has paid her dues when it comes to diving. Like many women, she was encouraged to go into a safe profession rather than follow her love for the sea, which has always been strong. She majored in and then taught English for six years before she gained enough confidence to break away to work as a dive instructor in the Bahamas. She's been in Bonaire as a naturalist and guide since 1981.

I had to recount the details of the dive again and again to Penny and Peter, who were completely fascinated by the story, and I promised them that they could learn to scuba as soon as they were old enough – probably around the age of fourteen.

Peter, especially, must have listened to Dee's stories carefully, as he found his own Moray eel living in the rocks at the end of the dock and was soon feeding it bits of hot dog every day and making a special pet out of an animal all of us would have shunned previously.

It was a delicious sight to see him perched on the edge of the docks calling out, "Mr. Eel. Mr. Eel. I've got some hot dog for you."

By the end of the week, the eel would come whenever Peter called – but not for any of the rest of us.

We would soon be at the end of our Atlantic Ocean trip, but the more we voyaged, the more we were finding there was to discover, learn, and enjoy.

And, yes, we had a wonderful Christmas, courtesy of Keith and Barbara.

STORYBOOK LAND

28

From Bonaire we made a quick day-sail to Curaçao, the second in the chain of ABC islands, the 36-mile passage taking only six and a half hours in the brisk easterly trade winds which blow with great regularity across the lower Caribbean early in the year. We sailed round the southern point of the island of Curaçao and began searching for the small opening to Spanish Water. I was doubtful if the narrow entrance I could see was correct, but a small powerboat roared past us and in, so we had to be outside the right gap. With the wind gusting right behind us, we took in all sail and with beach to starboard, rocks to port, and not much water in between, we motored slowly into the beautiful tranquil waters of this landlocked harbour.

Three weeks go by fast when you're anchored just off a pleasant yacht club, with friendly and interested members. Many international cruising yachts passed through and we caught up with old friends we had not seen since the Canaries. We spent afternoons swimming at the beach, or strolling about the nearby historic town of Willemstadt, a tropical adaptation of a seventeenth-century Dutch town.

But we wanted to spend time in the San Blas Islands, which form a long chain just a few miles off the coast of Panama, and had to move on. We would sail right past Colombia, for though some yachts do stop there now, most boats still avoid Colombian waters because of the country's rampant drug trade, most of which takes place on her beaches or just offshore. So, full of Dutch delicatessen treats, we prepared for the 720-mile sail from Spanish Water to the San Blas Islands port of Porvenir.

If ever we passed into a storybook land, a place strange and fascinating, it was when we sailed to the San Blas Islands of Panama. At times we felt like Gulliver, for the Kuna Indian inhabitants are a diminutive people, most of them less than five feet tall. Thought to be the last of the full-blooded Carib strain that inhabited the Caribbean before the Spanish conquest, they live along a series of tiny islands, reefs, and cays that spread for ninety miles along Panama's Caribbean coast, southeast of the Canal.

This proud but gentle matriarchal society is to be congratulated. In spite of the fact that the sophisticated Americanized civilization of Panama is on their doorstep, they have retained their land, their customs, and, to a great extent, their autonomy. If one wants to visit these islands by yacht, one cannot just check into Panama, one has to clear into the San Blas Islands themselves. The official is a Kuna.

After a six-day sail, we were glad to be approaching the islands at dawn, as it was difficult to make out exactly where the entry port of Porvenir was in the jumble of small islands ahead of us. This became apparent as we got nearer, but the waters were dangerously shallow and reef-strewn, the inshore currents were strong, and the recent wreck of a yacht to port attested to the potential danger.

Porvenir is a tiny island, only a few hundred yards wide and perhaps half a mile long, but even so it has the main airstrip in the area. Yachts have to take care to anchor clear of the runway approach as the planes using it come low over the water. Strangely enough, there is nothing but the Customs House, the airport, and a much-used fresh-water well on the island, though there was once a hotel here. The main population lives on the other three islands in this cluster, and a large village has grown around the casual tourist hotel on the island just across the channel.

The islanders have a good lookout system, though, and the entry of a yacht in Porvenir is a signal for the Kuna Indian women from the other islands to take to the water and bring along samples of their famous molas. The mola is the hand-stitched panel of cloth traditionally worn by the Kuna women, and is made up of three or four layers of cloth with a pattern cut and sewn into the layers. It is a sort of reverse appliqué, as the pattern projects *down* through the layers rather than being built up above the main cloth. No sooner was our anchor down than three canoes appeared alongside, all filled with friendly, brightly dressed women – and many children.

We had heard of the molas and were very interested in purchasing some of the traditional designs from the women. These designs of animals, sea life, devils, gods, and intricate centuries-old geometric patterns are dying out, being replaced by flowers, Superman, helicopters, and the Panama Canal! Ugh.

I hardly knew whether to look at the molas or the women. Both were beautiful. Though the molas are now made to sell to tourists, the women still wear them as everyday clothing with two panels in the same pattern used to make the front and back of a blouse. With their gold nose rings, head scarves and bead leg bands of red and yellow, and brightly patterned sarong skirts and molas, the women are a striking picture.

We beckoned the women and children aboard, and soon *Lorcha*'s cockpit was full of different women, ail eager to show us their work – and to see inside the boat. There was no overt competition, but we took care to buy one mola ($5 to $20) from each canoe. The more we examined the molas, the more we could see differences in design and craftsmanship. After we had

226

looked at about three hundred, I think I could tell a "good" one from one not so exquisitely fashioned, though some of the choice is, as ever, a matter of taste. I grew to respect the women who wanted $60 for a mola. It was usually an outstandingly fine piece of work and they knew it.

"We'd better call it a day," I said to Fiona after about two hours of mola examination. "I think that's the Customs man at the dock. We haven't reported in yet."

"It's Saturday," said the immigration officer in shorts and T-shirt when I presented our papers ashore. "That will cost you $10 per passport for checking in on off-hours."

"Would it be better if I came back on Monday?" I asked in hopeful Spanish.

The official smiled.

"If you would like to go to sea until Monday," he said, "that would be all right with me."

I could just see myself telling Fiona and Penny and Peter after a six-day passage that we were going to sea again for the weekend – and I paid our overtime charges with good grace. In fact, I'm not too unhappy about paying extra charges for formalities in remote islands, especially where we don't have to pay mooring charges. As long as the fees are reasonable, we don't find harbour dues or overtime charges something we should get upset about, although we have met many yachtsmen who fuss and fume unreasonably over the slightest "extra" payment.

Normally we avoid hotels and hotel meals. They're usually both expensive and bland, but even at a distance we could see that the local hotel across the water might be different. For a start, it had a thatched roof.

"Let's dinghy over and treat ourselves to lunch, Fi," I said when I got back from Customs. "Maybe we'll be able to get some fresh bread and vegetables, too."

The hotel proved to be one of the few hotels in the world where *all* the guests come by boat or dinghy. A few yachties like ourselves row over, while Panamanians visiting the San Blas

Islands for a day or the weekend fly in to neighbouring Porvenir and are then brought over by motorized canoe. The Kuna-run establishment was as casual as a small hotel could be and still function – and was a real treat. The large walled-off coral pool in front of the hotel served as a living larder for keeping fresh fish, and had the biggest lobsters we had ever seen. It was like a giant aquarium, and Penny and Peter had a great time reeling off the names of all the fish, much to the surprise of a couple of English-speaking guests.

The tables were set in rows, so that getting to know our neighbours was no problem. The open terrace looked ocean-wards and service was casual and friendly. On the day we were there, there was a choice of two plates – lobster or chicken at $6 and $5. Fresh bread was piled on the table, cold water was served in big jugs, and large, completely filled plates were set smilingly in front of us.

Day tours, with lunch at the hotel, seemed to be popular, but we were the lucky ones. We could wander round the islands most day-tourists get to see, but we also had the time and the transport to see the less-visited islands.

The major Kuna villages are on the Carti Cays, only about five miles from Porvenir, but there is no passenger boat service to or from the mainland. The anchorage at Tupu Tupila is well protected, however, and in the middle of the group, so it was here that we stayed for a few days to see Kuna life. The village has one of the seven major chiefs, a landing-stage for the inter-island trading vessels, and about three hundred people on an island that seemed no larger than one city block. The thatched roofs were thatch-to-thatch, and houses ran down to the water's edge, where some were even on short stilts.

Everywhere we went we were stared at, especially Penny and Peter, for though white people are not unusual, small Caucasian children are. Penny and Peter clung to us; they were not frightened, but they were taken off guard by the totally different culture, way of life, dress, and housing of the Kuna Indians.

"Hello, my friend. Are you American people?" said a voice from over the side of the boat. "Hello, my name is Jimmy."

228

We had been told about Jimmy Harris, a full-blooded Kuna Indian who had worked for the U.S. Army in the Panama Canal Zone in his younger years, and spoke English quite well. We had been hoping to meet him, as communication with the Kunas is difficult. Few of the Kunas speak Spanish, the official language of Panama, as their first language is the Kuna dialect. And even Spanish was not all that helpful, as I don't speak it very well.

Jimmy had the typically slight build, dark mahogany skin, black straight hair and short stature (about 4 feet 8 inches) of these people, and as he sat in the cockpit having coffee and a snack with us, we told him we wanted to see a cross-section of Kuna life. We asked if we could go up one of the local mainland rivers where the Kunas gather fresh water, fruit, and firewood and do their laundry. The burial grounds were also located upriver.

"Tomorrow we go up the river," said Jimmy. "With your outboard on my canoe, we can do the trip in a few hours. Today we go to my house."

We walked around the narrow streets and open houses of the village, Jimmy showing us where bread was baked and where we could buy dried smoked fish. We bought two fish and three plantains before going to his house.

"Take as many photographs as you want," said Jimmy, used to the ways of visitors. Normally, taking photographs is very difficult, as the Kunas don't like people taking their picture. If you point your camera down a village street, everyone disappears indoors in seconds, even when you think you're being unobtrusive.

"Twenty-two of us live here," said Jimmy as he indicated the one large room of the thatched-roof structure with bamboo walls. "But fifteen of them are children."

With Jimmy not working for the Canal Zone any longer, the men of the house would fish while the women sewed molas. This did not provide a very big income for such a large family. But not everyone thought in these terms. We asked one yacht who had been taken around by Jimmy what they paid him.

"Oh, nothing for going around the village," said the yachtsman carelessly. "But he did take me lobster-fishing one day, so I gave him a dollar. He seemed quite happy."

"You stupid, insensitive bastard," I thought to myself. "You take up almost four days of this man's time, he even shares his food reserves with you, and you give him a dollar. How far do you think you could take your family with that?"

We were looking forward to our river trip. But the next day Jimmy was a couple of hours late showing up. When he did come, he told us there was a funeral that day and so no visitors were allowed up the river. Too bad, as it would, of course, have been interesting.

But tomorrow, he promised, we would go with him and his son. But the next day was rough and thundery – so the trip was off again.

"Oh well," said Fiona philosophically. "Let's go and see if we can visit the island chief and perhaps take him a T-shirt."

Chief Johnny Smith was a genial older man with failing eyesight. He was delighted to meet us, and we were reminded that it was a good thing to pay our respects. We were invited into his home and solemnly presented with a god-stick he had just carved. We, in turn, gave him a red Toronto Brigantine T-shirt with a picture of a sailing brigantine on it. There was much smiling and touching of shoulders.

The next day we were astonished to see the old chief paddling his canoe out to *Lorcha*, just as we were going to eat some lunch.

"I've only got some bread and cheese," said Fiona aghast.

But she quickly brought out the salami we had been saving for a special occasion and mixed some cold rice and smoked fish in a salad.

We thought it was pretty brave of the old man to come out alone, as he spoke not one word of English or Spanish. Luckily, about fifteen minutes after the chief had been safely settled in a corner of the cockpit, another canoe came by, paddled by a man named Gerry. As Gerry spoke quite good English, we invited him on board, too, and we ended up having a fine and interesting lunch with the chief and our interpreter.

"Can you ask the chief if there is a problem about us going up

230

the river?" asked Fiona. There was a long exchange between Gerry and Johnny Smith. Then it came out. It seems that a couple of years previously, a missionary group who had come to the islands had gone up the river with a few of the local people. They had – oh, terrible sight – seen some women and children bathing in the river and had snapped pictures of them nude. These photos eventually showed up in the mission magazine as an example of the primitive and uncivilized lifestyle of the Kuna Indians, who obviously needed to be saved by Christianity.

The Kuna people were greatly embarrassed and rightly indignant about this episode. Since then it had been forbidden for foreigners to go up the rivers, except with the permission of all the chiefs of the seven islands in the Carti Cays.

Chief Smith gladly gave us his permission. That left six! You just can't hurry meeting and talking with chiefs, so reluctantly we had to scrub the river trip from our agenda.

The following day we sailed for the Chichime Cays and enjoyed some good diving and spear-fishing in what we thought were fairly isolated surroundings. There were only a couple of houses on the beach. At least, that's what we thought until a large tour boat turned up, looking incongruous as it anchored beside our island, disgorging about two hundred passengers for a two-hour visit.

Visiting the San Blas Islands had been lovely, full of interest and family fun. But it was time to be making for Panama and a decision as to how we would live for the next couple of years.

Would we head north and return to Canada – or would we sail through the Canal and head into the South Pacific?

We had left Toronto with the intention of voyaging for two to three years, and already twenty months had gone by. We could still make a leisurely trip up the eastern seaboard of the United States and get back to Canada in the fall and keep to our original schedule.

"What do you think, Penny and Peter," we asked at a family council over dinner, "should we go back, or shall we head for the South Pacific?"

Our two moppets had no idea of what or where the South Pacific was. They knew nothing of the distances involved, or the plans and charts necessary. The fact that we would be heading for the world's largest ocean was beyond their comprehension.

What they saw was a continuation of our Atlantic voyaging lifestyle. The boat, the sea, beaches, birds, animals, new people, new countries, and adventure on a small boat with their beloved mama and papa.

Could there be any doubt of their response?

"The South Pacific," they both chorused. "The South Pacific."

I looked at Fiona and we both smiled, nodding our agreement.

"The South Pacific it is, then," I said.

EPILOGUE

Committing ourselves to a circumnavigation was never in the original plan. We merely wanted to sail in the world's oceans as long and as far as it suited us. So far it has suited us well.

As skipper, I can say that I have become used to planning and making ocean passages of many hundreds of miles without undue concern. I do not expect easy passages, but I am willing to go to sea with our particular boat, with Fiona – who can stand night watches and reef the sail as well as any boat partner – and two small children, confident that we can remain safely at sea until we make a secure landfall. For *Lorcha* has proved to be a good home and a well-found ocean cruiser. She is seaworthy to the point that even in the heaviest weather we have encountered, she has inspired confidence.

I have learned to be content at sea, though neither Fiona nor I always find long passages a pleasure. Even though I know I have done my homework and everything will work out, I still get anxiety attacks when we are approaching land. At those times, Fiona is a tower of strength, giving me the confidence that we have made the right decisions in passage-planning, and being patient with me and allowing me my anxiety. I can sail thousands of miles without worry, only to be on edge for the last twenty.

Though the travel and exploration is something we all learn from, the formal education of Penny and Peter has been Fiona's responsibility. Even though correspondence education is time-consuming, Fiona likes the structured format it gives our lives, and the order it imposes on our otherwise informal lifestyle.

233

And the children? They love our life, enjoying attention from both parents all day.

In general we have found that boat children tend to be outgoing, well-mannered, and intensely curious about the world around them. Contrary to most people's assumptions, they are gregarious. They become accustomed to making friends in a short time in perhaps unusual circumstances, and are not shy around other children.

Early on in our voyage, Peter used to shout "I only speak English" to local children when they tried to talk with him in their language. Now he is much more tolerant, eagerly plays with any child he meets, and works hard to learn (and proudly repeat) a few words of that child's language.

Peter loves to fish, and though I am constantly untangling snarls from his fishing-line, it is instructive for him. He learns patience, and an understanding of marine life, and he already knows that food does not come from wrapped packets in stores. He loves to help around the boat and ties good knots.

Penny, too, is a willing and able boat person. She helps up-anchor, can take the helm, and sheets in the sail. She is a strong swimmer and can dive deeper than any of us, often diving to check the set of the anchor. She handles the dinghy well, and she and Peter will often row around a secure anchorage either for fun or to do an errand for us.

Both children show signs of developing into strong, inde-pendent, and resourceful young people, traits that as we con-tinue voyaging will develop further, to stand them in good stead all their lives.

As the parents of small children in whose company we live twenty-four hours a day, we have an interesting perspective on the world, seeing it as we do through the eyes of Penny and Peter. The main factor isn't just that we are in the company of our children, but that the surroundings for all of us are constantly new, usually stimulating, and often demanding. It tests all of us.

Having children on board ship has another advantage for the voyaging family. They are a common denominator the world

234

over, and when people in other lands see that we have children on board, they immediately feel at ease. Our cheerful pair delight in making new friends, and through them we often meet people we might not otherwise have got to know, or experience adventures ashore that may not come the way of a boat without young children aboard.

Though our lifestyle may be deemed somewhat unusual, we are still an ordinary family. Nothing makes things more homely and normal than catering to the needs of a small child. Penny and Peter may live unusual lives, but their needs are the same as any child their age – even though the "normal" child perhaps never has to try to use the toilet in a rough sea, or experience nightmares about sharks.

First the Atlantic – and now the Pacific Ocean.

Will the Indian come next?

At this moment we are secure as a family unit who are enjoying their current way of life. And for the moment Penny and Peter are content to voyage with us. We will keep sailing until we feel the need for a change.

ACKNOWLEDGEMENTS

We wish to thank Shelley Robertson, former Life Editor of the *Toronto Star*, who ran many of our Atlantic sailing articles under the logo "Family Adventure on the High Seas" from 1983 to 1986. This was the first regular sailing column of its kind in Canada and we were grateful to Shelley for her enthusiasm and insight. Thousands of people became interested in our adventures through these *Star* articles, some followers even finding us at various anchorages in exotic locations.

Thanks also to Percy Rowe, former travel editor of the *Toronto Sun*, who published articles on our 1975/77 European sailing adventures from time to time in the travel section of the *Sun*.

Material on our sea voyages has also appeared in various sailing magazines, including *Canadian Yachting, Cruising World* (U.S.), and *Practical Boat Owner* (Great Britain).

Toronto literary agent Lucinda Vardey encouraged us for many years to write about our voyaging experiences, and ebullient publisher Doug Gibson worked with us on the manuscript with his customary élan. His editing was fierce but friendly.

Contact with the many sailing yachtsmen who set out on adventurous passages before we did encouraged us to make our ocean-crossing dreams a reality.

All contributed in no small way to the publication of this book.

236

APPENDIX A:
Description of *Lorcha* and Equipment

KM-30
Designed by Frans Coblens of Amsterdam in 1977
Double-chine steel construction
Hull and decks built by Karmac Yachts, Hamilton, Ontario, Canada, 1979
Converted to junk rig and fitted out by Paul Howard
Launched in 1980

Principal dimensions

Length overall 29'3"
Waterline length 23'7"
Beam 9'7"
Draft 4'3"
Displacement (weight) 5 tonnes
Registered tonnage (a measure of interior volume) 7.19
Sail area 440 square feet
Mast, yard, and battens of aluminium

Equipment

Hydrovane self-steering gear
Engine
    Two-cylinder Yanmar diesel of 15 h.p.
    200 litres of fuel
Standard Horizon Maxi 88-channel VHF
Sestral Moore compass
Dinghy
    7'8" × 3'8", fibreglass construction, built by John Bain of Sault
        Ste. Marie, Ontario, to the Phil Bolger "Puffin" design
    Dinghy outboard: Seagull 40 featherweight 2 h.p. outboard

238

Anchors

    Main: 7.5 kilo Bruce on 200 feet of ⅜″ chain, with Simpson
        Lawrence Hy-Speed windlass

    Others, in order of most often used:

        35-lb. fisherman anchor

        Viking 5000 aluminium dismountable "Danforth" type
            anchor

        35-lb. Southwest Marine Factors plow type anchor

Galley

    Two-burner with grill propane stove with 20 lb. of gas in two
        tanks

    340 litres of water in tanks and jerry cans

APPENDIX B:
Itinerary

1983

July 1–August 4
Hamilton, Ontario, to St. John's, Newfoundland
Total distance sailed 1,500 miles

July 1–3
Hamilton to Kingston, with brief stops at Toronto and Picton

July 4
Kingston to Crysler Park, Ontario

July 5
Crysler Park to Royal St. Lawrence Yacht Club, Laval, Quebec

July 6
Royal St. Lawrence Yacht Club to Expo Marina

July 7
Expo Marina, Montreal, to Trois-Rivières

July 8
Trois-Rivières to Quebec City

July 10
Quebec City to Gros Cacouna Harbour

July 11
Gros Cacouna Harbour to Rimouski

July 12
Rimouski to Matane

July 14
Matane to Grande Vallée

July 15
Grande Vallée to Gaspé

July 16–17
Gaspé to West End, Prince Edward
   Island

July 18
West End to Cap Egmont

July 19
Cap Egmont to Charlottetown

July 20
Charlottetown to Ballentynes Cove,
   Nova Scotia

July 22
Ballentynes Cove to St. Peter's Port

July 23
St. Peter's Port to Baddeck

July 27–29
Baddeck to Miquelon

July 29
Miquelon to St. Pierre

August 1–2
St. Pierre to Bay Bulls, Newfoundland

August 3
Bay Bulls to St. John's

August 22–September 2
St. John's, Newfoundland, to Santa
   Cruz, Flores, Azores
10 days, 20 hours*

September 4–6
Santa Cruz to Horta, Faial, Azores
2 days, 6 hours

September 28–29
Horta to Ponta Delgada, São Miguel
1 day, 5 hours

October 7–13
Ponta Delgada to Funchal, Madeira
5 days, 14 hours

November 2–5
Funchal to Tenerife, Canary Islands
2 days, 15 hours

December 3
Santa Cruz to Las Palmas, Gran
   Canaria
11 hours

1984
January 4–12
Las Palmas to Mindelo, São Vicente,
   Cape Verde Islands
8 days, 2 hours

January 20–22
Mindelo to Praia, São Tiago, Cape
   Verde Islands
1 day, 23 hours

February 4–17
Praia to Fernando do Noronha, Brazil
12 days, 18 hours

February 25–27
Fernando do Noronha to Natal, Brazil
1 day, 22 hours

April 2–4
Natal to Areia Branca
1 day, 16 hours

April 6–8
Areia Branca to Fortaleza
1 day, 22 hours

*Times given for ocean passages are from secure in harbour of
   departure to secure in harbour of arrival.

April 20–22
Fortaleza to Luis Correia
1 day, 23 hours

April 24–May 1
Luis Correia to Belém
6 days, 23 hours, including anchoring
   three times (about twelve hours
   each) to await the turn of the tide
   to get up the Rio Pará

June 23–28
Belém to Cayenne, French Guiana
5 days, 7 hours, including anchoring
   three times waiting for the change
   of tide to get down the Rio Pará

August 9
Cayenne to Îles du Salut
7 hours

August 16–23
Îles du Salut to Scarborough, Tobago
7 days, 3 hours

August 27
Scarborough to Store Bay, Tobago
2 hours

August 31–September 1
Store Bay to Scotland Bay, Trinidad
14 hours

September 2
Scotland Bay to Trinidad Yacht Club,
   Port of Spain
3 hours

September 15
Trinidad Yacht Club to Trinidad and
   Tobago Yachting Association
2 hours

September 17
Trinidad and Tobago Yachting
   Association to Guiria, Venezuela
12 hours

October 1
Guiria to Cariaquita Bay
6 hours

October 2
Cariaquita Bay to Ensa Pargo
9 hours

October 2–3
Ensa Pargo to Testigo Grande
14 hours

October 12
Testigo Grande to Porlamar, Isla
   Margarita
9 hours

October 20
Porlamar to Cubuagua
4 hours

October 22
Cubuagua to Boca de Rio
3 hours

October 26–27
Boca de Rio to Isla la Tortuga
14 hours

October 30–31
Isla la Tortuga to Puerto Azul, Caracas
1 day

November 23–25
Puerto Azul to Las Aves de Sotovento
1 day, 13 hours

December 6
Las Aves de Sotovento to Bonaire,
   Netherlands Antilles
9 hours

1985

February 22
Bonaire to Spanish Water, Curaçao
6½ hours

March 17–23
Spanish Water to Porvenir, San Blas
    Islands, Panama
5 days, 21 hours

March 25
Porvenir to Carti Cays

March 29
Carti Cays to Limon Cays
3 hours

March 31
Limon Cays to Chichime Cays
4 hours

April 2
Chichime Cays to Porvenir
2 hours

April 3
Porvenir to Porto Bello
11 hours

April 4
Porto Bello to Cristobal, Panama Canal
    Zone
3 hours

APPENDIX C:
Factors in Choosing a Boat

A STEEL HULL

Lorcha was our fourth keel boat.

Our previous vessels, in order of ownership, were a 19-foot fibreglass-over-plywood sloop; a 29′9″ carvel planked-wood gaff cutter; and a new 21′6″ fibreglass bilge keeler with junk rig. And now *Lorcha*, a 29′3″ double-chine steel boat with junk rig.

The 19-footer was light and nimble, quite fast for her size and good fun to sail. We never did get an outboard for her but sailed her around Lake Ontario engineless.

We bought the heavy-displacement wooden cutter with diesel engine in England and sailed her all over Europe. *Seagull* was a lovely boat to look at, sailed well when there was a breeze, but was more work to handle than Fi or I like.

The 21′6″ fibreglass vessel was ordered new from the builders with the optional junk sail plan. She had twin bilge keels and an outboard auxiliary, and was relatively heavy for her size. *Lady Fiona* was a good vessel, carrying us some five thousand miles in all sorts of weather.

On our previous voyaging, we had seen wooden and fibreglass hulls holed and sunk. Our own wood- and fibreglass-hulled vessels were bashed about, and though we encountered no serious problems, there was a fair amount of cosmetic damage and potential for worse. I vowed that our next long-distance cruising vessel would have a steel hull.

Though steel hulls need more attention than fibreglass, they require less than wooden hulls. With modern paints – and *many* layers of paint – the problem of rusting is minimized.

Steel hulls can be made to be watertight. With her welded-steel decks, cockpit, and coach-house, *Lorcha* does not leak a drop. Fibreglass vessels flex in a seaway, caulking works out of the joints, the hull-to-deck joint begins to leak, and then the hatches begin to drip when spray and waves come on board.

Steel hulls are more abrasive-resistant than any other hull material. If you run onto coral or rocks and waves lift and bounce you, a wood, fibreglass, aluminium, or ferrocement hull is likely to be holed or ground away with the wave action.

We saw two fibreglass vessels sink in a Greek harbour. When the fenders collapsed in gale conditions, the hulls began rubbing on the stone quay. By morning the vessels lay on the bottom, with gaping holes at their waterlines.

An acquaintance of ours, Steve Saunders, was driven ashore in a gale on the west coast of Ireland. His steel-hulled *Wufflewood* lay on a windward shore pounding on the rocks for eight hours before he could get her pulled off. She lost lots of paint and had some dents, but she leaked not a drop.

Osmosis can be a problem on long-term-travelling fibreglass yachts; when they are left constantly afloat in warm tropical waters they can develop osmosis blisters.

Joe Silverman's Hinckley Bermuda 40 is now undergoing its third treatment for osmosis. The Amel Maramu 46-foot ketch *Cleve*, owned by Claude Vogt, had to undergo treatment for osmosis in her second year.

The procedure is to haul the boat. All underwater paint is removed, the blisters are popped, and the hull is dried out for about three months. Then the holes are filled and faired, and a new undercoat and bottom paint are applied. It is a time-consuming process, equivalent to wooding, refastening, and recaulking a wooden hull.

A rusty steel hull needs only sandblasting and priming, a few days' work, though this can, of course, be expensive.

If you are considering purchasing a second-hand fibreglass boat, power or sail, for an extended voyage in tropical waters, check it very carefully for osmosis blisters before you lay down your money. If the boat has been left afloat in warm tropical waters for a few years with no long-term lay-ups, it is likely to have some bubbly warning signs. Heed the warning.

Not that I am discouraging people from travelling in fibreglass boats. At least half of the vessels in any harbour where long-term cruisers (as opposed to local or charter boats) congregate will have fibreglass hulls. But recognize that the material does need extensive maintenance over the years.

DIRECTIONALLY STABLE, COMFORTABLE HULL

Any preference and/or choice of hull shape and type is very personal, but I will spout my own bias.

I feel that the heavy-displacement, long-keeled cruising boat is as much of a dinosaur as the heavy-finned, fendered big V8 road-hog cars of the fifties and sixties.

Boats cost by the pound, making heavy boats expensive to build and requiring large engines to power them. They may perform well in some conditions, but in light airs they are slow, especially if the wind is forward of the beam. They require heavy sails and sail-handling gear and take lots of work to keep them going.

Light, buoyant boats are easily powered by sail or engine. They cost less for a given length and are easily handled. The limiting factor is that light boats must be kept light. To load down such a boat not only presents a loss of performance, but can be dangerous in heavy weather.

Light boats can sail faster in light airs, will be faster and more comfortable in heavy weather when the heavier boats have to heave to, and will average more miles per day on an ocean passage.

Liberty of Norfolk, Virginia, a Bruce Farr 36, regularly made daily runs in excess of two hundred miles when crossing the Pacific. Our Australian friends Russ and Michelle on *Last Wave*, a Joe Adams 39, often have daily runs of 180–190 miles never flying a spinnaker or pushing the boat.

The above two designers, along with some of the newer Robert Perry designs, several French designers working with light aluminium and steel centreboarders, and some of Tom Colvin's light steel designs, typify this new breed of cruising boat.

If we were in the market for a new vessel at this time for a long-distance family cruise, we would look for a 36-to-40-footer of this type.

MULTIHULLS

Though I have had little sailing experience on multihulls, I always ask the crews of those we meet how they like their vessels. Many are first-time boat owners, though I have met some converted monohull sailors. I recall having spoken with only one former multihuller-turned-monohuller. His reason for doing so was, he said, "security".

Modern cruising multihulls do not average many more miles per day on long passages than modern monohulls, so speed is not a real factor. Most multihulls are slower to windward; that is, they take longer to reach a windward destination than do monohulls.

But the real advantage is that they sail flat. The old sailorly cliché of "rolling down the trades" takes on a new meaning to monohull sailors after a two-week dead-downwind passage. Monohullers arrive in port with muscle fatigue from constantly hanging on, whereas multihullers step ashore relaxed and ready to explore.

The multihull "flip-over" controversy is, I feel, overemphasized by monohullers. We have not experienced "ultimate" heavy-weather conditions, but I have no doubt a well-found multihull could have easily handled the rough weather we experienced.

Multihulls we have met are evenly divided between catamarans and trimarans. I like the look of the catamarans because of the interior accommodation arrangements, but both have advantages and limitations.

246

Preferred hull/deck material by the multihullers I have met is foam-cored fibreglass.

AN EASILY HANDLED SAIL PLAN

Lorcha is the second junk-rigged vessel with a free-standing mast that we have taken long-term voyaging.

There are several types of junk rigs. Our previous boat, *Lady Fiona*, was of the Blondie Hasler type, a yachty adaptation of the old working Chinese rig. This is a light and easily handled rig, all controls going to the cockpit, with no need to touch the sail when raising, lowering, or reefing. It is great off the wind, but slow to windward.

Lorcha was first rigged with the Gallant rig, designed by Jack Manners-Spencer of England. This is a foil-shaped, double-sided sail enveloping the mast. The attempt was to make a sail as easily handled as the Hasler rig but with improved performance with the wind forward of the beam. We sailed local waters with this system for two summers, but though it was faster to windward and the boat pointed higher, the rig was too heavy and did not control well when reefed to half or less of the sail area.

Before we left on this trip, we took off half the Gallant rig, changed the shape of the sail slightly to be something between Hasler's high-pointed sail and the Gallant rounded top, and rigged *Lorcha* as *Lady Fiona's* sail had been rigged. It is this rig that, at the time of writing, has propelled *Lorcha* 25,000 miles in all sorts of weather.

To be fair to the Gallant rig, Jack Manners-Spencer has since done a lot of development work to reduce weight and improve handling.

There are many other variations of the junk sail plan. Sunbird Yachts of England have developed a variation called the Swing Wing rig, claiming all the upwind performance of a sloop rig, the downwind performance of the junk, with the ease of handling of the Hasler rig. It is a good-looking rig and I would like to try it.

Tom Colvin of Miles, Virginia, is one of the best-known designers of vessels with the junk sail plan as an option. His rigs are single-sided and are close to the traditional Chinese junk, in the shape of sail and in the way they are rigged. His sail plans are worked from the mast, are self-tending, slow to windward, and fast off the wind, and are the simplest to put together and maintain.

Though the junk sail plan is often dismissed by local sailors who are into club races and beating to windward up the bay, it is a top-notch voyaging rig. When ocean-sailing, performance to windward closer than 55–60 degrees from the wind is not of paramount importance, as closer to the wind than that is so uncomfortable that few cruising sailors elect to try for that last ten degrees.

Lorcha regularly outsails other cruising boats up to six feet longer when going downwind, when the other vessel is not flying a spinnaker. Few cruising boats fly spinnakers even in ideal conditions, yet most trade-wind sailing is downwind sailing, where the junk rig really shines.

I know that the junk rig is not for everyone, but those serious about family ocean-sailing should consider this sail plan. The best source of information is from the Junk Rig Association, Hon. Secretary Peter Weigall, 16 Fairfield Road, Bosham, Chichester, West Sussex PO18 8JH, U.K. They print a bi-annual newsletter and have a worldwide list of members.

If you insist on having all those stays, expensive deck hardware, and half your stowage space filled with sails, most cruisers prefer a cutter rig, with roller furling/reefing on the outer jib.

RELIABLE DIESEL POWER

Though a few cruising yachts do manage without an engine or with just an outboard, I feel a good engine is a necessity on a family boat.

An engine is not just for use when manoeuvring in harbour. When in doldrum conditions on a long passage, the vessel able to power through calms may reduce its passage time by half over the vessel that lies rolling in the swell waiting for a wind.

There are many atoll and river entrances so narrow and with such a constant outflowing current that an engineless vessel could never enter them, and an outboard on a transom bracket would be dunked in the turbulence.

Engines are necessary for charging batteries. Though we have a solar panel which is sufficient to recharge the batteries in tropical sun conditions, sometimes the sun just doesn't shine.

A reliable engine of 2–3 horsepower per ton displacement, along with a first-class installation, will constantly pay dividends in terms of safety, convenience, and the resale value of the vessel.